Overview

Steven Berkoff is an actor, director and playwright. His plays include *East, West, Sink the Belgrano!, Decadence, Kvetch, Acapulco, I am Hamlet* and an adaptation of Kafka's *Metamorphosis*. His film credits include *A Clockwork Orange*, *Octopussy* and *Beverly Hills Cop*. He lives in London.

Steven Berkoff

OVERVIEW

faber and faber

LONDON · BOSTON

First published in 1994
by Faber and Faber Limited
3 Queen Square London WC1N 3AU

Phototypeset in Palatino by Wilmaset Ltd, Birkenhead, Wirral

Printed in England by
Clays Ltd, St Ives Plc

© Steven Berkoff, 1994

'Rambo: Acapulco'; 'The Fishermen: Acapulco'; 'The Town Square:
Acapulco'; 'On the Wrecking of the Santa Monica Pier by Storm' and
'Johnny Ray: Hollywood' originally published in *Steven Berkoff's America*
(Hutchinson, 1988)
'Hitler: Vienna' originally published in *Time Out* (1986); 'Greek' originally
published in *Time Out* (1988)
'Twenty Years of Metamorphosis' originally published in the *Independent*
(1989); 'Fiji' originally published in the *Independent* (1990)
'The New York Times' and 'The Run: New York' originally published in the
Guardian (1990)

Steven Berkoff is hereby identified as author of this work
in accordance with Section 77 of the Copyright,
Designs and Patents Act 1988

A CIP record for this book is
available from the British Library
ISBN 0–571–16981–3

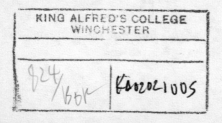

Contents

Introduction

The theatre has not only been a source of creativity over the years but has also acted as a magic carpet, transporting me and my works to the four corners of the earth where I have dropped my theatrical seed and have watched it flourish, or not as the case may be. Some lands were fertile and others were harder soil in which to bring strange plants to fruition. In New York, I saw no less than three of my own works struggle to penetrate through the tough pavement of the city and eventually wither and die. Exotic plants need special care and they found more welcoming soil and reached abundant growth in other lands. Paris in particular was a fertile climate in which the same three plays: – *Greek*, *Kvetch* and *Metamorphosis* found homes.

I started to record these events in the journal I always took on my travels and which also doubled as an ally in my shoulder bag; one I could always rely on to keep me company. It helped to distil the day's events and give them some cohesive form, enabling me to meditate on my actions and sometimes resolve thorny problems. Many a lonely night was transformed into pleasurable solitude by the presence of my notebook and pen. A journal also acts as a kind of camera recording the environment in which I happen to have landed. This is its most pleasant function, since I've always liked taking photographs and bringing back memories of wherever I happen to be, as if there were a compulsion to record every day of one's life, lest it be lost forever.

I have sat writing in cafés in many cities of the world, since the café, bistro, diner or bar is a good place to write and be outside and yet still be in the stream of life rather than in the confines of one's hotel room. I have written on beaches in Brazil, Mexico, Sydney, Bali, Nice, and in small diners in New York, sushi bars in

Tokyo, beer kellers in Munich and so on and so on, since the pleasure of eating or drinking coffee seems a good partner to the act of writing. This is why so many of my impressions feature the café I am in.

In New York, I became fascinated by a small diner on Third Avenue. It was a simple, lively place and had a remarkable atmosphere; a Norman Rockwell painting brought to life. I felt that I needed to set it all down, as if I could paint it and all its occupants, but the next time I came to New York it had disappeared from the face of the earth, with no memorial to say that Arnold's Café had sat here for forty years, fed thousands of satisfied customers and had been a creative force on the great lined and scarred face of New York. So, this is my memorial to Arnold.

Film also has transported me to many lands, but then I have usually been a passenger on somebody else's carpet. The experience, of course, is less intense than the experience one has when facing the responsibility of creating a theatre work that will have an impact not only on the actors and audience but, as theatre can, become for a time part of the bloodstream of that city. One is part of that city, that organism, and has the intensely privileged position of being suddenly thrust deep into its heart, since for most nations the theatre is its emotional profile, the image it wishes to present to the world. If one succeeds in touching the nerve of a nation, it may have reverberations for many years after the event.

I have been fortunate enough to have theatres around the world show my works and often have directed them. I have witnessed them bear fruit in revivals over the years but, more importantly, have seen them read, studied and used by actors to sharpen their teeth on. Most of these essays take place in the USA, and I was always glad to have been invited, and privileged during the time of Joe Papp's administration, to the New York

Shakespeare Festival. He asked me to direct *Coriolanus* at the Public, something that in England would be as likely as flying to the moon. I went at it with a will, and it became my contribution to New York at the time. I was glad to have my Sunday in the country with Joe Papp.

In the end a journal is a kind of personal way of reacting to an experience; and, like a storyteller, one must involve the listener and take them on the journey. I hope the reader enjoys the trip.

Steven Berkoff
15 March 1994

Rambo . . . Acapulco . . . 1984

After a stint on my first Hollywood movie, Beverly Hills Cop, *I was immediately relegated to the 'villain' category and given another Russian heavy to play. Stallone himself asked for me, having originally cast me in* Beverly Hills Cop *until he walked off the project – and so I found myself in a hurricane-torn, swampy Mexico waiting for the weather to clear. It was an eight-week stint, but I managed to squeeze a play out of the situation, and some Mexican impressions.*

As I awoke from a wretched slumber dreaming that I was drying on stage, the phone spluttered into life. I was to get on the set immediately! I rushed to the breakfast that was being laid on my sea-view panoramic balcony and wolfed down my croissants and coffee whilst eyeing suspiciously some ragged grey skulking clouds stealing some thunder in the distance. The sky had been torn apart by recent hurricanes and still looked bruised and bloody. I pulled on the thinnest T-shirt I could find to counter an expected hundred degrees in the Mexican jungle.

The air-conditioned cars sped us to our location. I hadn't worked in a week in this hurricane-blasted Acapulco – it was possible to sit by the pool ordering countless Margaritas until you were called. For the stunt-men this was like being let out of school, and they swarmed all over the pool, and the available girls, making lots of noise and discussing overtime. For my part, I learned scuba-diving and even water-skiing in a local lagoon which looked like a backdrop for paradise. I was getting a touch of Montezuma's Revenge brought about by an overdose of dodgy fish taco washed down with Mexicali Beer. I wasn't in the mood for work. There was a lot of hanging around while Stallone and the director debated the day's shoot, and I was reading *The Conquest of Mexico* by Bernal Díaz. Treacherous Spanish dogs, giving the Mexicans glass beads in exchange for gold and conning them with Christianity served with smallpox. The Kray Twins, along with Charlie Richardson, were jailed for life for what the robbers Cortés, Raleigh and Cook were given Royal Estates for. Thieving and plunder has to be sanctioned by the state. So, throwing all these thoughts aside and ignoring the lines of begging hands and wide imploring eyes, we sped down the main street, Acapulco, which is very pleasant, lined with great monuments to the gods like the Acapulco Plaza Hotel, which is cunningly shaped into an Aztec 'Cue' or temple. These vast

3

temples engorge live tourists, brown them first by the pool, accept their tributes . . . play some loud garish Mexican/American music and spit them out again after a beer contest and aerobics daily. I had been growing a tumour of revenge as I stared down at their porcine bodies in those modest long swimsuits shouting and splashing at their hideous daily volleyball in the pool. The only sign of the Mexican revolution was a street we passed called Emiliana Zapata Street . . . and photos of rifle-toting dark figures in huge sombreros that could be bought in the boutique of the hotel.

The set was a tropical POW camp where I was a Ruskie officer of sorts, flown in to interrogate our unusual captive. The rest of the POWs looked realistically starved and chancrous, an eerie sight first thing in the morning . . .

Our car had sped through the suburbs of Acapulco, past dozens of little stalls mining a small seam of a livelihood selling coconuts and candy. The contrast between the natives and the visitors is appalling, and the babies lying dozing on the laps of begging mothers whose day is earmarked to a piece of pavement presented a sight that the Aztecs had eradicated 500 years ago, before the fag-ends of Europe showed them civilization.

I was by this time sweating buckets, and the heat-blast struck me full in the face as I left the air-conditioned taxi. I sped to the little 'Honey Wagon', or dressing-room trailer. It's called 'Honey Wagon' since it is like a little cell, but the only thing you produce in there isn't honey. The Aztecs had little huts along their highways and actually recycled excrement and thought it quite valuable. I was called on the set to join a swarm of people including technicians, actors playing Russians, Viets, POWs plus wardrobe and hairdresser who seemed to spend her entire life adjusting the way 'Sly's' hair would flop over his forehead after he had been submerged in the slime-pit. When not doing this there would be a lot of intense talk amongst make-up and wardrobe about the restaurant the night before. Others were now

4

milling around, including stunt-men, stand-ins, extras – and there was Stallone, almost, as he stood on one crooked knee, like a familiar statue in Florence. He was wearing little bikini pants and waiting to be submerged once more in the slime-pit. He was covered with mud, and adorning and sticking to his body was a collection of hand-made leeches. He was lowered into the pit in a kind of leather harness and hung there, waiting to be raised, like a piece of cooked meat. And I, svelte, cruel, cunning Ruskie, am about to interrogate him. Movie realism demands more than Bogart's action in *The African Queen* when he flicked the damned leeches off. No, I take a sharp knife and dextrously slice the nasty slugs off, leaving behind a red splodge, courtesy of 'props' . . . the heat of the body against the rubber leech ensured that the stage blood looked runny and viscous. We did that a few times and then broke for lunch, which was really good homely Mexican food. We were given T-shirts advertising the movie. It had Sly on the front, muscles bulging and about to pop and veins swimming under the flesh like snakes while grasping an M.60 machinegun as he blasts villains away. It is a marketable formula that he not only gets away with but does well. He co-directs, writes the script and part produces while at the same time creating a body out of hundreds of mind-numbing and punishing hours in the gym. This regimen makes him a hard taskmaster. Technicians or actors not up to par are flown in and out with the frequency of auditions . . . we are on our fourth cameraman in as many weeks.

Paranoia gets to you, and every phone call by the production office had me mentally packing my bags. The heat today blasts over the forest, and vast multi-coloured butterflies flicker like kites over the grass, vultures hover above and exquisite dragon-flies in gunmetal blue dart over the small stream that runs through our artificial village. We do the take. The sweaty first assistant director, David, an Englishman, is one of the discs in the backbone of England, since although boiled like a beetroot he none the less commands with easy authority a motley assortment of Italians, Greeks and Americans. He is totally unflustered and humorous, as if to suggest that, while it is beneath his dignity normally to associate with such scum, he will nevertheless bring us through battle and on to victory. The second assistant, Roy, hardly ever sweats, and I see now that the English inflexibility is their power. They cannot blend, they bring England with them, and even if it is a hundred degrees outside, inside their minds it is still Pinewood Studios. David doesn't even step into the shade as we all do for a few seconds. There he is, Captain Hornblower, or a great English whale spouting up great geysers of sweat.

We deposit the multi-million dollar body once more in the pit, and once more I descend from the chopper through lines of 'Russian' soldiers standing to attention as I stride in. The Russian sadist I play is accompanied by a Mongolian giant, who keeps claiming to me that he can fight anyone in the world, and that it is unrealistic for Stallone to beat him in the film in a straight fight. I explain that this is movies but it obviously bothers him a lot. When not preening himself on his martial attributes he hunts down 'pussy' and avails me of all the details of the prior night's conquests. It is a fascinating act, as it is accompanied by much gesture and sound effects. Slide my knife across Sly's stomach again and he pulls back sharply . . . oh my God! I've made contact with real flesh . . . I prise the horror off, and behold, his flesh is intact and firm. He is *acting*! It certainly gives me a scare.

The Fishermen . . . Acapulco . . . 1984

Most days I didn't work and would walk along the beach trying desperately to find something to do to make my time here worth while. I saw the fishermen there each day and was fascinated by the chain of bodies linked together in the almighty effort to pull the mystery out of the sea. One day I decided to join them.

Watched the nets being drawn in this morning, and the boys and men became a fresco of bodies leaning into the shore and moving together one step at a time. They were a reflection of the sea's power and the weight of the net. The net was slowly being drawn in by inches, suggesting some great bountiful catch, when in fact the length of rope which dived into the sea and then out to the nets made the weight considerably heavier, that and the dragging of the nets across the ocean floor . . . so they leaned on their heels and heaved the slow-moving burden with its mysterious contents being gradually and systematically trapped . . . the figures pulled against the life in the net, pitting their bodies against the water-soaked ropes that held the condemned fish. The ropes were twisted round their shoulders and then entwined round their backs, and then pull, pause and step . . . I wanted to take the rope for a while, as if to contribute and make their struggle that bit less, and whether this gesture was guilt or just curiosity I didn't know, but they received my offering with friendly smiles and didn't seem perturbed by this bloated red-faced tourist wishing to touch and be part of this ritual. I became a link in the chain at Acapulco, a chain that had been going on for centuries. After a while the effort became enormous . . . they really were putting all their strength into it. My hands were red and being rubbed raw by the rope. I turned and saw that they had twisted the rope around their bodies in such a way that they were using their bodies as the pivotal force and allowing their body weight to fall back. I leaned back also, but still had to grip and pull, although with slightly less force than before. So for a while I was 'pulling my weight', which was no doubt appreciated, since any effort of mine must mean a bit less for them. For the first time I had a clear meaning for the metaphor 'pulling your weight', and of how fishermen must trust their colleagues to do so lest they subsidize them with their own precious strength . . . and how galling it is when your own limited energy is used up the faster because someone is stealing it from you. I wanted to stop; I had made the gesture, but now I wanted to carry on with my walk and leave them to the pain that was a daily ritual in their lives. I walked on a while and watched from a distance. The net was now almost in, and part of it was being folded as it was dragged up the beach, and the contents were still unknown but the dark, slowly diminishing shape held a certain magical excitement, for you still could never be sure of the surprises nature could stun us with. Now they were bringing their nets closer and there was a slight movement on the surface of the water as the life within was becoming inexorably trapped. Small ripples broke the surface, and now other, non-edible, life might be trapped in the same net and then die for nothing but that's the way of death. You cast your net and it may trap some undesirable elements.

Now there is a crowd of people beginning to form some back-up action by standing behind the nets and preventing the luckier fish, which may have leapt out of the net as the water became shallower, from escaping. At this point the breakers are pouring over the nets and some of the fish are pouring over the side with them, so these dozen or so men and boys are armed with plastic bags, hoping to act as a kind of barrier. The bags are regular shopping bags, and are of different colours, and so form a kind of fisherman's flag. They are excited, for it seems that what escapes is a kind of bounty, or perhaps it doesn't matter too much since the larger fish will invariably be trapped . . . or perhaps it is even a ritual that has been going on for centuries, whereby the people get their 'perks' from what they manage to scavenge. The nets are now being pulled into the shore and the crowd surges in, greedy for the Pandora's Box to be opened . . . they must see the mystery of what the sea offers even if it is more or less the same thing each time; there is something thrilling about catching and exposing what is normally hidden from the human eye. These are things from another environment, and they carry some of the mystery of the environment with them. Not the same with hunting game that you can see on land anyway . . . here you do not see it until it is brought in . . . and then there is the awe of watching something live pass into death . . .

Here there is still the thrill of owning the sea. It is the last thing that is left for the poor. There are no walls and boundaries for the simple fisherman. It is moving and thereby unclaimable, and what you pluck from it is yours. You can rob, steal and plunder, for it is only your patience that you have to sacrifice, and in a poor country the sea is an endless treasure chest. The fish are like precious jewels and silver crescents and they gleam like the money that they will indeed fetch, if the catch is big enough . . . glistening and flickering in the sand as they are trapped by the nets, the bright, iridescent shapes squirming like sunlight playing over broken glass. Or diamonds. And it is not a bad catch. The large 'restaurant fish' are placed in a pile and are blindly leaping into the air or frustratingly beating their tails into the sand, and what was clean and brilliant is now dirty and sand-clogged, its pearly translucent skin becoming dull and pathetic. It seems a sad death, gasping its life out in a squirming pile. Then the smaller fish, as thin as playing cards and square like silver ceramic tiles, are also flickering like leaves tossed in a gust of wind. What good are these, I think. Why not toss them back? But these were thrown into a plastic bag, no doubt useful for something, maybe soup, since they are thin and fleshless. And now the nets are giving up the rest of their bounty plus the debris of this filthy sea at Acapulco, which seems to resemble a disgusting overflowing toilet since the nets have dragged in a tangle of old rotting refuse.

There were bits of ragged toilet paper that had not disintegrated and other junk in states of semi-decomposition, and wriggling tiny fish were being unpeeled from the mess as if the fishermen merely took for granted the polluted sea that the hideous growth of tourism had bequeathed them. They merely prised the tiny moving bits of life from the junk, as if it too were

11

simply the bounty of the sea. Some fish were rejected outright and thrown to one side, where they were now in danger of being trodden on, including one small plump fish with whiskers which was maybe a catfish. I watched the scrambling naked feet and willed them not to tread on the small live pumping thing that was attempting to bury itself in the wet sand. I couldn't somehow interfere with this ritual and stride out and at least throw back what was not wanted. The nets were now being folded and I was in the way but I took this opportunity casually to walk over and pick up the little fish that had been left and, like a bored tourist, throw it back into the sea. Its little fins spun into action and it whisked off into its familiar terrain. A second one I tried to revive merely puffed for a while and turned over, too far gone to recover, but I was glad for the one that got away, and trusted its fins to hit the water and not air as it dived and felt the sanctuary of its sea home. Then I saw a young boy do the same. Maybe he was watching me, and no matter how pathetic may have been the gesture of rescuing some piece of life that was not wanted, he was sufficiently influenced to do the same . . . he threw it into the air to reach the receding breakers, and that trip I think would not have been too healthy for it. My fish swam off, and who cares about one fish, but it was a small and intricate life that man will never reproduce, a miracle of creation. There was also lying on the sand a huge swollen white fish with spikes like a porcupine and distended to its utmost limit to frighten its prey, and nobody wanted it. The strongest image was all the fish that were fighting for life and slapping the beach and hurling themselves into the air, but there weren't in the end enough to fill a large suitcase. It had taken all but the best part of the morning to haul the nets in and there were at least six men to pay. I had learned what 'pulling my weight' was, anyway.

The Town Square . . . Acapulco . . . 1984

I wandered around Acapulco much of the time alone since the others were generally working. Being alone gives you more time to reflect and ponder on the smallest details of life and to meditate on the lives of others. Loneliness also does have compensation in rendering your senses more alert, as if they were in a state of perpetual hunger or need.

Sitting in a warm town square where all the world comes to mingle at the end of the day, I feel protected, as if this were the town's sanctuary. The stone figures at the end of the square watch over us, ancient Indian heroes from Aztec history. The atmosphere is warm and soft and the square becomes a womb where everybody drifts at the end of the day and sits under the large trees or on the stone walls surrounding the fountains. The big old chestnut trees shelter us and kids are leaping around the square playing tin whistles and chasing each other round the fountain. In warm countries the square is such a haven, a bath of warm human contact where you can dip your tired spirit. Where in England can you do this? Just wander in a town square and be able to merge into the life-flow of the people and be replenished by it. The British have no harbour, only a dank and fetid pub. But leaving these damp thoughts aside let us drift into the perfumed air of the square.

By some trees in the centre there were shoe-shiners, a group of men earning a living, the smell of their polish and wax sending a pleasant fragrance through the air. There were at least five of them and each had an alloted niche which they will perhaps occupy for life. So I had my shoes shined that had run on wet tar-stained beaches and dusty roads and had never felt the soft embrace of leather and wax on their dry and frayed skin. The shoes were stained and the man worked hard to remove the tar marks and I sat and floated in the gentleness of the square where thousands have dozed off before me and allowed myself to drift in the sensation of fingers gently patting and stroking my feet. I didn't feel any sense of his abjection or my patronage . . . it was just a job and I was only a pair of feet that had walked for miles that day and his hand seemed to restore some life into my concrete-pounded ends. Poor feet, that had thirteen stone crushing them down into a relentless walk. I sat and tried to compress all the details into my head, I was already making a verbal *enchilada* out of the experience. I didn't even let it cool and savour it later . . . no, even then I knew I wanted to write it down since I was in literature while I was in life.

His shirt had a neat crease, so maybe he had a wife looking after him, and the faces of the men shining shoes had an immense dignity undiminished by the task they were doing. Their faces in no way showed any lack of higher intelligence or that this simple work was their only vocation. They looked as if they could equally be doctors or lawyers, which is the patronizing way we have of looking at things, since we come from a land where opportunity has at least some semblance of being democratic.

Here, where poverty is rife and corruption manifest, an ordinary decent human being could easily end up being a shoe-shine boy for no other reason than his honesty and lack of guile. These people were clean and neatly dressed and looked like they carried their weight and others' in the world.

He was now working at a piece of tar-like substance . . . I felt his hand battling with the elements that had stained my neglected shoes but he did not give up. Different bottles were being chosen and brought into the struggle and strong smells drifted up into my nostrils and it smelt like the most fragrant perfume.

The smell and the soothing effect of his hands combined to send me into a tranquil and benevolent mood and I watched the leaves barely tremble on the tree as the twilight settled into the square. It was filling up now with after-workers and school kids and couples sitting silent and holding hands, and old men sat on the fountain's edge and swung their legs. The church bell now sounded the half-hour and told the kids how long they had left before rushing home for dinner. The man was finishing off my shoes with a cloth that he unrolled like a bandage and was whipping around my heels. He found a resistant stain and searched his cleaning cloth for a relatively under-used piece to apply some more cleaning fluid. He stretched the cloth out and searched the whole of it like you do when trying to find a dry spot on your handkerchief for a runny nose . . . he did this with great concentration, turning the cloth this way and that, and seemed unable to find a dry or clean patch worthy enough since my shoes were of a cream-coloured leather and he had to be more careful than usual not to rub some other stain in. Eventually, and this took some time, he found a sufficiently suitable two square inches, wrapped it around two fingers in a swift motion, which made a kind of hard and secure surface, and worked the stain out. It was as if he was looking at the map of the world . . . the cloth. His tenacity impressed me. He seemed totally engrossed, searching and moving it around its four corners, turning it over, and all the while his face expressed nothing but the decision of doing the job to the best of his ability. There was no forced matiness and no humble pie. It was a matter of fact. He finished, and it was sixty pesos . . . which today is thirty cents. I gave him a hundred pesos, fifty cents . . . but that didn't really seem enough . . . but what would be? Only my changing places and doing his shoes would be enough. The poor, or call it the third world, has been cleaning our shoes for years and it's about time we took our turn . . . When it comes, I hope I shall do it with the same stoicism.

Johnny Ray . . . Hollywood . . . 1984

I was here performing in Decadence *at a small fringe theatre in Hollywood. It was my first performing stint in the USA although I had had several plays on. I played in a seedy part of Santa Monica Boulevard where the sad males would hang out trading their bodies. Nobody likes going to this part of town, and even in this squalid dump seating ninety-nine people we didn't do that well, but managed to get through eight weeks. I loved it, since we only played Wednesday through Sunday and had much time to see other things – Johnny Ray was one of them!*

Entered this club called 'The Vine Street Bar and Grill' expecting to see in the flesh someone who travelled through thirty years of time with me and came out of the tunnel on the other side. What did I expect as we both crawled through the space of memory called the fifties? I was curious to see what it had done to him. The winters then seemed brilliantly cold and the steps of the London Palladium were choked with Crombie-coated teenagers like myself. My hair was curled into a soufflé of Brylcreem and the collar of my shirt rolled away like a giant wave so that any gust of wind would have had me airborne. It was in fact called a Johnny Ray collar. It was the generosity of the collar and its creamy expanse that contrasted with the dull British two-inch collar in a desperately dreary post-war world. He came out, according to memory, thin and shiny, and his suit glistened. His sun-coloured hair casually falling over his face. Androgynously, he appealed to us all. He was male and female in an easy flow between the two, like the girl who plays principal boy in panto. It was sweet. He was hypnotic to the fourteen- and fifteen-year-olds whose sexuality was still forming in the crucible of adolescence. He formed no clear image which might threaten us to emulate. He was not a heavily sexual Frank Sinatra or a greasily gross Frankie Laine or wholesome Guy Mitchell. Johnny Ray was eerie . . . spaced out into a world of pure emotion, his music was full of dissonances and yearning tunes. It haunted and possessed us and could even be demonic. His voice flew like an arrow directly into our emotion. It was the cry, almost a primal cry of pain. The letting out of the high tenor notes crawled into our young ears and found empathy, responding like a dog responds to the high-pitched whistle. It was intended for us alone . . . He cri . . . ee . . . iee. . . .ied for us. We also yearned. We were not cuddled, like our coarse elder sisters, by the sexual syrup of Sinatra's 'Foggy Day in London Town', to be heard in front of the fire with their spotty teenage boyfriends while they exchanged their over-fulsome gropes, and we were out in the cold. We had Johnny Ray . . . like a winter blast. Ray was his generation's Bowie. His repetitive warbling note was a mantra to us . . . like he was climbing a flight of stairs and, reaching the top, shared the view with us and then we slid down again. It was the moan or the call!

'I . . . if . . . your . . . or . . . swee . . . eet . . . her . . . art . . . se . . . ends . . . a letter of goodbyeeyyyy.' It's the pleading downbeat, the crawling for love and affection, the begging. He was begging, on our behalf, armed with his props to conquer the dragon that was the audience – his spear was his deaf-aid, and the lank blond hair falling over his eye, the thin body striking angular movements. All conspired to win us, since he was us. We were flawed and incomplete. Sinatra was already there, conquering women, whereas Ray was continually failing and therefore like us! 'Broken Hearted Now' . . . It was not only the sanctuary he offered to our still struggling sexuality, it was as if he was beyond sex and offering up sweet and sad emotions as surrogates. The words were blatantly naive and innocent. 'Talk to her please Mr Br . . . oo . . . ook . . . speak to her Mr Rainbow and take her under your branches please Mr Tree . . . ee . . . eee . . .' Nothing sexual, but even more powerful, since he evoked tenderness in us – 'a little white cloud that cri . . . i . . . i . . . ied'. Naive and yet beautiful in the innocence of fairy tales or children's book illustrations . . . pastel colours and soft landscapes . . . branches of trees . . . 'Walking my baby back home, arm in arm over meadow and farm walking my baby back home . . .' While in fact we were walking in Dalston, Hackney, or through the grim Orwellian council estates of Finsbury Park, where the lifts when working were used as a convenient urinal. 'We'd stop for a while, she'd give me a smile and snuggle her head to my chest . . .' The brutal gropings of early sex behind the council blocks. 'We'd started to pet, and that's when I get her powder all over my vest'!!

Nothing more nor less than the sweet image of make-up and powder. We longed for the next song.

So here I was, thrown from 1954 to 1984. I was working in Los Angeles on a movie with Eddie Murphy and my local paper advertised Johnny Ray at the Vine Street Grill, a small bar restaurant which lay at the vital intersection of Hollywood Boulevard – who hasn't heard of Hollywood and Vine? Did I not get the same mythic longings when I was in Delphi as I did when I crossed Sunset Boulevard? They stayed like ley-lines in the unconscious, bred into our memory banks in the warm cocoons of the Odeon when we were barely past walking age . . . and had we not yearned for that escapism ever since? And here I was at the centre of it. And a myth was singing, live! In a crumby little bar just off Hollywood Boulevard . . . Was an aged Odysseus running a tavern in Corfu? It would have felt the same. I heard him before I entered the club, which was a reasonably popular drinking tavern and restaurant seating about forty people with another couple of dozen in the bar. I turned up early for the second set and was shocked at hearing his voice at the entrance of the club, the disembodied voice searching through the speakers disturbed me enough to ask the girl at the box office to get it turned down. It was as if time and space made a sudden contraction. 'The amp's far too loud for that song,' I pleaded as if awakening from a deep hypnotic sleep. His distorted voice spilling out on to Vine Street had reached into the distant past and collided with my memory of him, which was purer no doubt than his own of himself, since repetition had coarsened his delivery over the years and I still harboured the early pure one at the London Palladium. Untouched. A perfect reproduction lay in my head like a pristine record. Why? Because we would impersonate him, not for any desire to act but for the sheer pleasure of letting our voices go and fly as he did.

I was an emissary carrying the tapes of the past. Anyway the girl agreed with me and said she would get it turned down slightly, as if any paying customer now had rights over his body and voice and merely for the asking . . . so low had he sunk to be within mortal touch. I was still as concerned for him as if the last thirty years that had separated us had vanished. So it was a protective emotion that he had inspired in us, and that still invoked the same loyalty as if I had at the same time been protecting the seventeen-year-old who came to watch. I wanted the image made secure, to see him just as he was. He was after all singing the same songs. So I walked in and came face to face with my past.

He sat on a stool right on top of the audience – mostly middle-aged – wearing a three-piece suit in a dark shade which neatly disguised a reasonable corpulence, and he was beating this particular song that I remember him singing to two thousand at the Palladium. But then I was sitting far away. Now I could see him, close up, like going to the fringe theatre where you are always intimately near the action – so intimately at times that it takes a while to get into the play, so forcefully are the actors thrust at you with their pulsing veins and fidgety hands. And so it was with him. He sat feet away and played the London Palladium. But even so he did not disappoint me . . . I had come prepared to make quick adjustments to my old vision and so allowed for his weight and the over-stressing of a song he must have sung ten thousand times. In the second set he strode on perfect . . . young-looking, radiating an innocence all the more poignant since his years had more than doubled, yet it shone through, even if he could not conceal a certain weariness. His hair was still blond-looking and fell over the side of his face, and he was still singing the memories of the past. I sat and allowed him to pull the years away from me and the other middle-aged in the audience for whom he was the touchstone of their youth. They went to the Vine and Grill to excavate a piece of their past that remains the same and is taken out from time to time to disturb the memories. The picture may fade and crease slightly, but the power of its ability to evoke is undiminished. We were feeding him with our memories of him and he was merely there to remind us. Yet he had a dignity one didn't anticipate, for he sang with all his might and passion as if he had just written the damn things and ignored those unfamiliar with the legend who ate and talked through his act! His eyes scanned the empty tables, which were more plentiful for the second set, and so he concentrated on a small knot in front of him and delighted them, as if they represented his world. I was not disappointed.

Those songs came rushing back like a great gust of wind, carrying with them indefinable clues and colours of hot, rabid teens . . . and the faces of history came into my view again. He was singing 'My Old Gal' and 'Broken Hearted Now', and nothing had changed. His repertoire had remained the same, untouched. He didn't 'cry' so much, but still was moving and took charge of the audience's emotions like a good guide taking them down Memory Lane. He still had the deaf-aid and seemed unworried about revealing that he had to adjust it from time to time, when his hand would sneak inside his coat and touch something situated near his heart whenever he finished a song. I suppose that when he belted he turned it down, unless he was testing that his heart was still working. Suddenly he had finished, and the audience warmly responded as if we had all been present at a seance to invoke the spirits of the past. I had to tell him about 'our connection' at the London Palladium. I went backstage to his dressing-room, which was shared with all the other musicians. He seemed distant, as I had caught him between 'time' – his place was on the stage and I had ventured to expose the mystery. He was just putting his working jacket on a hanger and I could see that he was even more comfortable than I could detect under the lights. He seemed pleased to receive my information, though I could see that everyone had a memory of him, from Hoedown County to Bethnal Green. He confessed unexpectedly a slight sense of shame when I mentioned the London Palladium, and said simply, 'This is an "off the wall" place to be in.' I had blundered by coming backstage and should have realized that performers would rather be seen in the bar in the safety of the atmosphere of the audience, since he had made for the bar after and was visibly far more at ease there with his fans . . . I left and walked into Hollywood and Vine, and the crossroads of the entertainment industry. I had taken a friend who was born after Ray 'officially' had finished, and she said, 'What an extraordinary man.' I was well and truly chuffed . . . or my seventeen-year-old self was . . .

Hitler . . . Vienna . . . 1986

They were casting War and Remembrance *in London and I knew I would play Hitler. I had to play it, for whatever reason. I felt I could create the monster. I met Dan Curtis in a London hotel, who expressed some doubt when he saw me, but after I changed into the wig and moustache and did my reading in front of his video he was convinced. It was the most satisfying acting work I ever did on film, and Dan would smile his craggy, big-toothed smile of appreciation after each take. He thought I was OK and said, 'Steven, you're a fucking great Hitler.'*

I'm in Vienna to play the greatest villain of all time: Adolf Hitler, formerly Heidler and descendant of Schickelgrüber. Hitler spent five years in Vienna in doss-houses and other flea-pits and I think it was in these dunghills of human vagabonds that much of his philosophy was culled. The type of person forced by circumstances or otherwise to live in these conditions is not tolerant of society or apt to analyse their condition. Argument is fierce and opinions are rigid and expressed with the subtlety of truncheons thwacking you across the head. Reduced circumstances lead to reduced opinions in many cases. We know that some of the most ardent socialists are frustrated capitalists, and that under-employment breeds strange bedfellows. Hence the inordinate amount of actors supporting quasi-socialist groups in this country.

Everywhere I go I sense his presence – the Opera House, the Burg Theatre, music halls playing light operettas of Mozart. Felt his presence in the Schubert Ring, and drinking coffee in the Schwarzenberg Café when he could afford a splurge . . . oh! – those marvellous Viennese coffee houses where coffee is served on a small silver tray with a glass of water . . . and you can sit for hours . . . civilization. After Vienna, London seems a slightly sick city, even inhuman as you enter the local tavern after work and the barmaid in tight ski-pants dribbles, 'Nah, we don't do food nights,' to a group of hungry actors after a rehearsal at the Half Moon Theatre . . . as if food were some kind of luxury not meant for the working classes. But you can booze yourself to death with impunity – in Vienna there would not be a tavern *allowed* to serve only booze – with the ghastly sound of a slot machine in the background where some yob dully and mechanically feeds his ten-pence pieces in the hope of Nirvana . . . YAAAAH! . . . for four weeks I never saw one of those ghastly machines that line every pub in England to make up for the loss of revenue or the loss of spirit by the owners.

In Vienna every café was an experience, and each one catered for people as if they were half human. I sat and thought about the role. Opposite the café was a sign giving the direction to Linz, Hitler's town where he grew up. So Vienna was the big city, where he was rejected. Rejects often turn to a political party or fringe group in which they can express their venom and poisonous frustration. Or they will form one. I imagine him staring into the windows of the Mozart Café and watching all those elegant and desirable ladies sipping their coffees and wolfing down their Sachertortes – those wonderful tarts . . . and the Jews!! – also sitting and eating with their families or going to the synagogue in the Judengasse in their strangely elegant costumes. So many of them.

Berchtesgaden, his weekend relaxer, his Brighton. Bormann, his mate, built an 'Eagle's Nest' on top of the mountain. It is still there, strangely enough, waiting for the Führer to return. You approach by a tunnel blasted out of rock and there, in a round chamber, is an elevator whose shaft has been bored through another three hundred feet of solid rock. The lift is steel and brass. He was in here! I am now seeing with Hitler's P.O.V. There are mirrors in the lift and red seats, and yes it is the original lift. I almost cannot believe what I am seeing as I am elevated to the top of the world. A remote, round stone room with a gigantic fireplace at one end framed in black marble. People have chipped bits off in the past. Now it's a café for tourists. But for two days it becomes the Eagle's Nest again. You feel as if you are floating at the top of the world. I am photographed where he stood. There is a magazine for sale to visitors full of photos of the previous tenants. There is a cosy one of Eva Braun warming herself by the fire . . . all so cosy . . . relaxing in Berchtesgaden when the killing became exhausting.

Hitler reminds me of a gangster who surrounded himself with sub-educated runts, like Bormann, Streicher, Goering, Roehm. Gangsters are attractive since they preach violence as a solution to problems which otherwise might take exhausting hours or years of negotiation. Violence is also attractive since you don't have to go to university to study it. It has a healthy smell . . . and it covers one's own fear or doubt. Gangsters bestow on their naturally weak underlings a sense of power. Their shadow casts a reassurance over their pathetic coven of yeah-sayers. Violence seems to attract always the extreme right-wing, whether in the USA, France, UK. It is decisive and requires little debate, and the fag-ends of Left and Right are characterized by reducing everything to headline philosophy and cant.

Hitler kept ranting on about Lebensraum. This living space for his German hordes. Why more space? He seemed to have tons of it. Nobody thought about it too much since it revived a dying economy. To acquire living room you need more arms; therefore more factories, more workers, more raw material. You don't care if your troops freeze to death in Russia since there are millions more where they came from. Violently inclined people always put ideology before human beings, and it's usually the ideology of race, i.e. fear of your daughter marrying a wog. Or land – fear of the wog buying it. It seems to be a deep-rooted fear, this land, race, nation, number – leading even someone as apparently educated as Enoch Powell to inspire violence by throwing matches over inflammable areas.

Hitler had some public works done and revived the economy by pushing the war effort to massively increase his army . . . and with all those fancy costumes the tailors were working overtime. But in the end, so what? He was a fraud. A gangster who used the methods of robbery with violence. A political Capone. I hope I never see the time when the world's values are as sordid as when it could participate in the Olympic Games in Berlin the year *after* the infamous Nuremberg race laws, which deprived all Jews of their rights and citizenship, though many had lived in Germany for centuries! Thus we and others condoned his crime and sanctioned it . . . even anaesthetized it by appearing at the

Games. Weakness encourages gangsters. It reinforces them in the correctness of their practices. Like a lot of bullies and gangsters Hitler raised his voice when thwarted. Its deafening tones camouflaged its lack of ideas or reason. No dialectics . . . just the shouting hysterics of the evil child who must not be denied. Screaming, table-thumping, whining, raving, apoplectic, insane, always right. The righteousness of stupidity, doss-house philosophy, fake ideology, ill-digested Nietzsche.

The director Dan Curtis says, 'Let's go again.' The German actors view me suspiciously. An Englishman playing Hitler? I get the wig on, false jowls, and then the famous signature – the moustache. I become him and he me – the symbiosis of the actor with his part. I walk on set and everybody quietens down. This is not a likeness. This is he. An actress, now an extra in her sixties, gasps. 'It cannot be,' she says. 'The likeness is extraordinary.' It's frightening. I look in the mirror and no longer see myself. He has returned. However, I begin. I am nervously apprehensive in this mixed English/German production with our cod Ya Vols! I am working opposite distinguished German actors like Wolfgang Reichman (Germany's Ralph Richardson) and Hardy Krüger as Rommel. First I have my scene with Rommel in which I chastise him. I start slowly, and explode into a rage. It is totally believable according to Dan – I have to feel so much hate, so much rage, frustration, insane disbelief at the actions of underlings. I've been here before somewhere. Instead of generals and foreign politicians I substitute a few critics. My rage comes out in an undiluted stream of pure bile. I have the cutting edge. Years of practice.

Hitler would weep at the sentimental movies he would show in his house, feel the greatest love and sentiment for his dog Blondie, above any human except Eva Braun who was a kind of lap-dog anyway. Sentiment is usually the nauseating side-product of the unintelligent and violent. It is a reverence for the harmless things that cannot injure them, like sad puppies in pet shops and weeping children on Christmas cards.

Mums and old relatives come in for this overwhelming reverence bordering on mania: witness the Kray twins' obsession with Mum and dear old Auntie. Anyone who can fend for themselves is a threat since all life is in opposition to the criminal, the gangster and psychopath. The Mafia gangster is different in the sense that he loves what is closest to him, for in a way since they are not against him they must protect him. Mafiosi are able to chop their victims to bits and then, after washing the blood off their hands, play with their friends' babies. Mrs Thatcher was able to call out a substantial amount of planes to search for her temporarily lost son, but summarily gave the order to sink a shipful of one thousand mothers' sons. This ship, as most of us know by now, was, contrary to the report in Parliament, *not* sailing towards 'our boys'. In fact, whether you agree with this decision or not, the facts are that it was not a spontaneous kind of World War II response on the spot to a U-boat attack. This ship was trailed for two days first. And the decision was taken after lunch. It was a very pleasant lunch, I believe.

Hitler would condemn millions of Jewish children and others like gypsies and Polish Catholics to die in a heinous way, while he played sweetly with Goebbels's children. I understand more and more what Jesus says when called by his devoted mother to come home – 'I have no mother' – or words to the effect that we are all brothers, and any injury to my fellow man hurts me. When people can separate only what concerns their immediate family from the outside world then we are in trouble. I have noticed that Reagan peppers his public statements with the magic word 'God', which he really believes injects his sterile philosophy with some moral values. He does this while supplying arms to overthrow the elected regime of Nicaragua which replaced the old gangster regime. The overwhelming evidence available in America of the Contras' atrocities of rape, torture and mutilation are ignored as long as they are not happening to 'Nancy'.

Hitler succeeded because everyone outside Germany was sub-human, anything not German was fit only to serve. Women were fit only to bear children. It was a simple philosophy that worked. Hitler's ideology removed the necessity of communication and collaboration. It stimulated Germany out of its rut, since all can jump on the Rambo wagon. Violence attracts a weakened society. Hitler knew this instinctively. Every street-corner runt who is leader of the pack knows this. Because force reaches down into the last member and last corner of the realm – its message is not lost on children and animals. It needs no analysis. It is irrevocable. Also it moves at a tremendous pace. It gives people 'protection' . . . and who doesn't want to be protected at times? Also, what unites Rambo, Reagan, Hitler, Mussolini – and I am afraid Thatcher as junior member – is that violence is *Big Box Office*. The only fly in the ointment is that you have to keep finding enemies . . . or you may have to invent them.

Zagreb . . . 1986

After work, ranting as Adolph during the day, I had great pleasure wandering around at night in the city of Zagreb, where I fell by chance into the most wonderful of restaurants, which was unlike anything I had seen in my life. It was what a restaurant should be – a sanctuary, a place of amusement, sustenance, camaraderie and joy – sheer, unadulterated joy!

Walked in this beautiful place filled with young people who look fresh, unspoiled and loll outside their café drinking coffee or beer. The life on the street so much more civilized than ours with our emphasis on booze. Our tavern owners obviously have never been abroad in their lives since they could not possibly sustain their antiquated and smelly boozers if they had. So I found a restaurant which seemed very homely and had that inviting smell to it . . . I wandered in through a bar which provided a friendly little annexe for people to meet and drink without necessarily eating, and then into the crowded restaurant itself where families seemed to be gathered for their weekly feast since it was Saturday. Each table seemed alive, with its members comprising their own flesh and blood – therefore one seemed to be inside a gigantic home. We in Britain don't believe in eating with our families except at home. We would rather eat with business colleagues, girlfriends or other 'couples' . . . the notion of your mum and even grandmum plus a couple of kids would be anathema. The family in poorer societies takes on greater import-ance and becomes the focal point for one's existence. The wealth of the family tree is in its branches. It's what one lives for and over whom one agonizes. And whose existence one celebrates by dinner out once a week or month, and sing, drink and eat.

As I walked through the various aromas I felt I was walking through their sitting-rooms and through their lives, so intimately were they enjoying themselves. Small groups were singing, swaying together or just bursting out, leaning over each other for support. At one end, three musicians were serenading some customers, a group of men who were singing endlessly.

I ordered my food, aware of the boisterous din behind me and wondering what were the songs that floated so effortlessly out of their mouths like a never-ending tapestry . . . as one finished another took over . . . perhaps as long as they were singing they would stay alive! Perhaps like Penelope, whose weaving kept her unwanted suitors at bay, just so their songs kept them on guard against other devils. Maybe they were old 'ethnic' songs passed down, since they all knew them so well. Yes, they must be songs of the people, of their folk lore or even their struggle . . . or perhaps not. Maybe just the equivalent of 'My Old Man's a Dustman'. The melodies were strong and drawn out and the three musicians, who now seemed totally commandeered by this group of about a dozen, were playing with greater zeal since after each bout one of the men would tip them. The three musicians were dressed in white shirts and flowing trousers ballooning at the knee and tucked into their boots in typical Croatian style. They played three different string instruments and one would play alone for a while and then the other.

The music was the paste of the culture that united them . . . it was as natural to them as food and drink, taken for granted, the result of a good meal, the treat afterwards, the release or tribute to the gods for the very feast you have enjoyed . . . the songs were shouted, teased, abused, ripped apart and wept over . . . the song supplies the fuel for all occasions.

There is a moment when the drink sets off a spark, the music touches a favourite chord and a grown man sings in the company of his friends and in full view of the restaurant as naturally as eating and drinking . . . he gives release to passions and the meaning of his life, his desire to be and to give . . . to put his emotions in a structure that will express the sheer joy of what he feels. The song and, more, the singing will 'say' everything for him. As well as entertain his mates. I understand now 'Wine, women and song', singing as important as sex. You embrace your friends with your song and give of yourself to them, and sometimes together you embrace the same song linked in a brotherhood.

The music went faster as the players too were demonstrating their own virtuosity, and now the diners were leaning on each other or resting their heads on the chests of their friends and even kissing each other's cheeks as they sang, arms around each other's necks . . . or they would pull out some paper money, roll it into a tube and stick it behind the ear of the player, not to disturb him while he continued playing. The men looked like ordinary simple workers, they looked as though they worked with their hands, since they had that exercised look and animation in their faces which I do not see in people who sit in offices. I was moved by seeing this expression of sheer joy, which of course may only be their fortnightly 'do' . . . the singing rose and fell and I continued eating, occasionally turning round as some guffaw signified some outrageous piece of buffoonery going on. They looked like a scene out of a movie, a celebration before catastrophe, innocence enjoying itself, in the safety of their own brethren before wars and politics, church and country claimed them. To take arms against other men just like yourself . . . men caught in the memory of a million other celebrations when you are so positively yourself and alive, protected that night by the food and the music . . . it could and might go on for ever. The full purpose of one's being: to be, and to sing. This had been going on for centuries, this simple celebration of man without interference of boss or guilt of church. Mates together, omnipotent and fuelled with their song.

I realized that I had forgotten what this was like. That in England this scene would be impossible. That no one sings in restaurants and you would be kicked out of a pub for causing a disturbance . . . unless they had a licence of course . . . or the sick spew of 'pop' continually regurgitating yesterday's gormless and anal twerps' lyrics.

We see music in the nodding robotic heads to the latest 'Prince' or other vague claim to music. Nobody sings any more but you might be 'screamed' at from an over-amplified mike in some grotty pub that in its desperate need to stay open invites groups to sing that would have been kicked out had they entered the place in balmier times.

In Zagreb I watched these men dragging out their souls, their childhood and manhood, their country, language, myths, and they were radiant. Perhaps the songs *were* the equivalent of 'My Old Man's a Dustman', but I doubt it . . . the music was too rich and too diverse . . . these were the songs of the country and its people. I could have mourned for the life I never saw and that was lost for ever. After 'All Things Bright and Beautiful' at school there was a void. We Brits have been emotionally castrated and any show of passion or any passionate feeling for anything is embarrassing. (I do not deign, when speaking of Brits, to include our far-from-repressed Irish, Welsh or Scots colleagues.)

Oh God, I had no songs in me. When someone asked me once to sing at one of those parties when everyone has a go I fled, excusing myself, and escaped into the Finchley Road. I felt like a criminal who might be found out. I had no songs in me!! When I left the café they were still singing.

Dinner in Cannes . . . 1987

I was sitting in my Brighton flat when my agent in LA rang and said jump on the plane for Cannes – Terence Stamp had walked off a film that 'Prince' the rockstar was making for his directing debut and called Under the Cherry Moon. *The film was a first-class disaster. However, I duly jumped on the plane and stepped into Terry's old clothes – Cannes was very nice. But as usual I found myself alone and reflecting on a piece of fillet steak.*

Dinner last night after a late September swim was wonderful. I found the right corner in the restaurant – one has to be comfortable – a well-located seat with a good view. Not too near anyone. I ordered, for a change, *filet au poivre, haricots verts* and mixed salad. The tablecloth was coloured in pastel stripes and the head waiter deliberated in front of me, and every choice I made was . . . '*parfait*' . . . flattering me as if my judgment reflected the discriminating standards of a gourmet. I settled down with the evening, enjoying the succulently cool air washing over my tight, sea-washed skin.

The French bread arrived first, with the *vin*, naturally. The *pain* was fresh and crisp, brown and crusty with a very moist interior that had the flavour of sour dough . . . I hate the texture of *baguettes* when they are dry. My half-bottle of 1981 *rouge* of unknown vintage was uncorked, and I supped it, and it was as only French wine *could* be that's bought and drunk in France – and in the South of France too . . . and in the open air at that. It tasted earthy, fruity and mild, with no trace of that acidy tang you get in London when you are unsure whether it's quality or crap.

It tasted perfect, as it should, better than those expensive decanted wines at the Connaught – because you should drink wine in its original country and not in swank restaurants in New York and London. No; they must be drunk, preferably in the open air, with crispy moist French bread, on the Riviera, on an evening in September when your body has been washed in crystal-clear waters and the night slowly turns from lavender to violet. Then it 'tastes' . . . so I drank the wine of Burgundy and it slipped down very easily . . . like liquid earth.

I waited some time, allowing my patience to be tested and stretched before I received my simple dinner – nothing fancy drowned in painful sauces but simple and wholesome, the obvious French dinner. At last along comes the steak and it *is 'parfait'*, sitting there swaddled in a simple pepper sauce which is coated in some unknown ingredients, like perhaps cream and herbs and of course peppercorns which have been crushed into the sauce. In a separate tureen sit perfectly cooked *haricots verts*, just springingly lying there in heated garlic butter . . . and a salad which is being tossed after careful removal of the sliced tomatoes on to another plate. The salad is robustly tossed in a delicious French dressing and the enlivened and glistening green sheets deposited on to the white plate. I take my well-sharpened knife and slice the steak – 'Its blood runs free, raw as a wound, soft as a kiss' – well, not so much blood since I ordered medium-rare, but delicious. The sauce in which I cradled my segment of meat had an almost malty as well as peppery taste which was also sharp, and yet was cushioned by the cream from attacking one's palate with too much ferocity.

I crush it between my steel-capped molars and grind away with my incisors and swallow it down followed by a cascade of wine. *Parfait!* It's hot and tasty and done just right, and the taste is mixed like the wine with open air and the soft luke-warm breeze. The meat hits a zone of memory and discharges a warm glow of earlier meat-eating times. Now hardly ever; but at this moment it gently runs along all those nerves and cells that eagerly respond and yield to the furious embrace of protein. I slice once more and reveal its pink centre, and the *filet* doesn't collapse after the first assault but still stands supreme and proud: dense-packed meat. It is determined to stay crisp to the last slice. Seeing this apparent integrity relaxed me enough to lay my knife and fork down and survey the work. So unlike your British restaurant, where the meat would already be collapsing in resignation and its forlorn state would require – nay, even demand – the constant attack with knife and fork so that the flourish of weaponry might disguise the tawdriness of the meat's performance. A good steak should preserve some structural integrity to the last slice.

Now it is necessary to survey the battlefield, to enjoy and feed your eyes while the stomach is busy sorting and identifying its new treasures. It looks good. I lean back and photograph it in my mind. Who needs company to interfere with this ritual? The steak is a third devoured. The remainder stands with shorn-off side, not ragged, but clean like a stone newly broken revealing the perfect smooth core. For a moment it looks like the cliffs meeting the sea at Sussex, but less crumbly; they resemble a side of Cheddar, but the steak looks *parfait* as the tide of gravy gently licks at its base. It needs no co-star. The *haricots*, which are beautifully cooked, are transported to the plate and instantly dashed to pieces in a basting gravy, and the *filet* once more is centre-stage.

The restaurant, like a beacon of warm light in the twilight, is claiming its customers, who sit wherever they are placed and fill up the little spaces like crossword clues. A couple with a child sit across the gangway and the nasty little brute keeps sticking her tongue out as if this were some kind of mean achievement. I ignore her after a few retaliatory lingual thrusts . . . and now an older couple have the temerity to be seated at the table right next to mine. Right next to me! Well, in France people don't mind such proximity since eating rules communication. I decide to engage the salad in a little side-distraction and pull out the larger leaf of lettuce, which now resembles a piece of green velvet, and the dressing is . . . *parfait* . . . rich, garlicky, and just enough mustard to make it interesting and attention-grabbing and a perfect contrast to the *filet*. Before returning to my '*amour*' I nibble quickly on a torn-off fragment of bread, just to absorb the slightest tingling on my tongue from the vinaigrette – just to make a bridge so to speak between the salad dressing and the steak sauce, not to confront them and create war on my taste buds. So the bread keeps the two adversaries apart in their more piquant extremities. I slice the steak once more and it's still holding on to its heat and I crush it with as much fervour and passion as the first slice when we had just met. This is a relationship that will not fade after the novelty of the initial excitement; in fact it is increasing, and I eye with a certain amount of comfort the remaining sizeable portion. It will sustain further assaults and not be demolished. The wine is still releasing those rusty hinges and pleasant day-dreams are being released from the stump of memory.

Something pleasant about being alone, if you do not gaze into paranoia, watching the world holding hands and families chattering like monkeys. If you can be quiet and calm within yourself it is like watching a movie. The absurdity of human behaviour is undiluted by the diversion of company. The world seems like a mad-house and the more trivial aspects of human beings are viewed in sharper focus. Here, now, the dinner is my companion and ally . . . my sole joy and friend . . . my only hope . . . my restorative, my amusement, my art and, most of all, my entertainment. I watch a woman opposite chipping at a hard red nail and for a moment I ponder the need for these fingertips that seem dipped in gouts of blood. It occurs to me that while the human body is subject to the ravages of time, much like a fruit, nail is hard and imperishable. It gives these women a sense that something within them is hard, firm and durable. For a moment I ponder the chef in the kitchen, since we never seem to think of them now, but I wish to imagine backstage with its haste and preparation, its medley of shouts and curses. I turn back to my plate, my wine and my salad . . . all grown for me . . . all destined to arrive at this particular point in time . . . all containing the elements of the earth and sun. I finish the steak and I finish the dinner and like an old friend my companion for the evening rests in peace reconstituted inside me. I pay the bill . . . 'Ca va, monsieur?' the head waiter routinely demands . . . *'Parfait.'*

Godot in New York . . . 1988

I was in New York having the time of my life directing
Coriolanus *for Joe Papp at the Public Theater. Chris Walken*
was Coriolanus and I found a theme that seemed to take hold. At
night we might see the odd show but the Godot *was a must –*
the 'hot ticket' in town, and being a staff member of the Public
enabled me to get two house seats. It was a greatly entertaining
night although sitting next to a director (Mike Nicholls) had a
deterrent effect; directors watching their 'babies' are notoriously
fidgety – he was no exception. Apart from him I enjoyed the
evening.

Tore along to this vast complex called the Lincoln Center and like most people arrived with two minutes to go only to face the vast quadrangle with ne'er a sign in sight, so raced across the square like a frenzied squash ball identifying all the buildings until some uniformed guy leaning against the wall guided me downstairs to the Mitzi Newhouse Theater. The buildings here seem to be landed with the unfortunate and unprepossessing names of their bene-factors, whose only contribution to the arts was unloading some unpaid profits, inspired by a little guilt and a desire for self-aggrandisement. I suppose the buildings could not have been graced with the names of the great in the same way as our Victorian empire builders blessed their theatres with the names of Booth, Barrymore, Garrick. But Mitzi Newhouse? And who the hell is Cottesloe? So I entered the Mitzi Newhouse, even if my tongue felt reluctant to put that sound on it, and sat down, grateful to have made it after a horrendous cab journey wedged inside a street of tin and carbon, cursing the minutes, since this was the town's 'hot ticket' and I couldn't be late! These tickets were impossible to get since the event was in the nature of a freak show. Two of the world's funniest comics deciding to redeem themselves and purge their sins in the cultural baths of Beckett. The giant Pan Am building impaling Park Avenue was my constant backdrop as we inched slowly forward toward our destination, and I tried to take comfort in its gargantuan aspect as it cradled the Helmsley building beneath.

I watched the people coming in and these seemed to be 'subscribers' . . . i.e. not real people who go to the theatre but people who support institutions and buy wholesale (five tickets for the price of three) and are on mailing lists. These support the theatre in all its worthy dullness and keep out the punters when there is really something to see. They are essential for the survival of many subsidized theatres and write complaining letters if their taste is being neglected.

Godot is fascinating when you get over the idea that it is 'significant', since it deals with a process of thinking that free-associates, so one could be watching an impro between two highly skilled comics, which one in fact does. Since there is no plot (i.e. an action which brings inevitable wealth or disaster) Beckett is able to write as a doodle and see what happens 'if' . . . to put two characters on the stage who are opposite in temperament and strike sparks off each other's differences; two minds collide in space. A limbo where all human distractions and material comforts are removed in order for us to see our naked core. Not for Beckett the absurd trappings of bourgeois comforters and trivial power games. We are made to confront both our essence as well as the void. Here we are close to Kafka . . . 'Man cannot live without a lasting truth in something indestructible within himself.'

Kafka prunes down everything to its naked core leaving us to contemplate the essential being. Beckett does this in *Godot*. He spits at the world's trashy obsessions, even if *Godot* is a four-star hotel compared to later refinements and privations in plays where blindness gives way to immobility and later to bodilessness. So these tramps still cling to the last memories of the whole body, still yearn and hunger and have not yet given up the chimera of things that might happen if we wait long enough. They feel all the frustrations of passing time without the little toys that enable us to feed the gulf of our existence which stretches out before us and which could be filled with the excitement of living. One must not confuse the genius with which a writer expresses the sterility of his existence with a philosophy of nihilism containing nuggets of revelation. A mother of a child, who goes to work, struggles for survival and watches her issue grow, relishing in the wonders of life, will have a different view from the life of a writer, childless, uninvolved except in the semantics of words, puritanical and cautious, staring before an empty page. Whether or not the conjecture of Beckett's life is true, the monastic acolyte will reflect quite differently our existence, and yet we are tempted to applaud the universality of his thought. I was never tempted to act or direct his work, much as I admired his craftsmanship, since there is a predictability to nihilism and its dour messages make for dour theatre.

But this is not the case. Forget those hairy Beckettian evenings at the Royal Court or Riverside and take yourself to this small horseshoe cavern called the Mitzi Newhouse (what a sweet little girl Mitzi was) and witness two of the best comics alive playing Beckett as if they were improvising the text. Great comedians contain a seismic needle which trembles at the slightest tremor, and there is Robin Williams's antenna quivering, nostrils flared to catch the merest scent of laughter, which he homes in on with his killer instinct. He tortures himself for a laugh as if laughter is contained in every part of human existence and needs to be wrestled out of it. An actor has a character to play and it doesn't matter whether you do or don't get a 'laugh', although actors are notorious for, once having found a laugh, defending it to the death. 'You're treading on my laugh,' as if the bubble of sound rising from the throats of the audience was the sure identification that the actor had found the Holy Grail. Apart from Robin Williams and Steve Martin, a real actor comes on stage who is doing a character and thus distorts the play. F. Murray Abrahams, a skilled New York actor and award winner, must have looked good on Mike Nicholls's casting sheet but, obviously over- whelmed by the sheer surgical skill of the comics, he goes for the jugular of the character and nearly strangles it to death by smothering it in a heavy Italian accent so overdone that the Robin Williams character is able to lick up the excesses in mocking impersonation.

Interestingly enough, the two comics used no accent but played in their own voices, speaking simply as themselves and conveying the text with crystal clarity. They appeared awesomely relaxed and produced a diction rarely heard from actors, as if they were compensating for the fact that neither had been on a straight stage in their entire lives! It was a compelling evening and the directing, such as it was, seemed clear as the figures acted their lives against a burnt-out sky surrounding a deserted wasteland.

The subscriber audience guffawed away in impersonation of canned laughter at each bit of 'funny biz' by Steve Martin, who was looking for fleas, smelling armpits – and the irony of watching millionaires playing two filthy tramps to a subscriber audience paying thirty dollars for the privilege. This same audience will fly out of the building past the 'real' tramps who, looking not that much different from those on stage, will beg for a little 'change'. The real tramps will be brutally ignored and left to die in the sub-zero New York street. I fled with others past the tramps and headed for a diner and bathed in its fluorescent warmth. I heard voices . . . 'You don't have raisin toast?' It was said in a way which implied that the customer's will was supported by such structures as raisin toast. It was a whine of disbelief mixed with anal need. The waitress apologized as best she could to appease the wounded beast. For those who are given everything such an omission could be serious.

Pilgrimage to Cannes . . . 1990

I have never in my life spent a more weirdly, fascinatingly bizarre two days. It was beyond anything I could imagine, and I was deeply grateful for such an essentially surreal experience. So much did I enjoy being out of reality that I returned the following year, that time to promote my own film, which of course, like most of the others, just didn't get made.

Decided at the last minute to visit Cannes, since the idea of a weekend in the UK locked in with the Sunday papers was more than I could stomach – and anyway I fancied a taste of France.

You can actually taste and smell France. It exudes itself into your nose and pours itself into your eyes. So what if the extreme Right dig up Jewish tombstones – they *do* make wonderful croissants. Anyway, I have a theory that countries that are overwhelmingly concerned with food are highly susceptible to the fear that others may want a share of the banquet. The promenade is graced by a procession of young beautiful women swinging their long exposed legs like scythes cutting down the ageing hustlers, who buckle at the knees as they pass, unless like me they happen to be sipping cappuccino at the Carlton Terrace in a comfortable wicker chair to watch the talent pour by. So distinctly unfair that women are expected to be young and sveltly attractive, with minor allowances for some maturing, but men need merely to be rich and active in the media and to be seen to be driving their films to market like wealthy bedouins with their fat sheep. The stars' faces are thrust into the air on high poles like Roman gods. They grace the giant movie houses, the temples of the worshipping masses, for this is the Mecca where the devoted come to worship and be worshipped. Stallone, Eastwood, Baryshnikov, Hackman, stare down at us, proud and obdurate as if carved for ever in stone. The actual physical enlarging of the actors' faces seems to deify them since they are seen to defy the laws of nature and are expanded to proportions larger than life and in the movies transcend all laws of time and space, protean beings with voices amplified to sound like trumpeting elephants. No wonder they are called stars, since they are transformed into other material that is unperishable. They await the time when they must tread like Agamemnon the red carpet on the way to self-worship at the 'Palais'. They slowly walk through the divided wall of human flesh held back by ropes, like some bulging waist held back in a belt from unloosing its sagging load. They await the time when an army of lower orders who are merely the priests of the temple, the photographers, guide their lenses to capture them for ever and minor starlets will be known to beam and have orgasms as the mute explosions of a hundred lights stroke their faces, and they hear the clicking of a thousand shutters which is like the tongues of a thousand men on their bodies. How they beam and part their mouths in rapturous ecstasy at the thousands of unimportant people straining for a glimpse. However, now the world converges on Delphi to await the verdict of the oracles who sit in judgment and will award points for style, content and transcendental illumination. I am staying at the Carlton Hotel on the first floor where all the rooms have been converted into small shrines to the deity of their choice and worshippers are sought to offer their oblations to the gods of Orion, Hemdale and Manifesto, whose leading prophet, David Lynch, is being acclaimed as the new Messiah, *Wild at Heart* is tipped, and of course is canonized by the prophets sitting on the jury and now blessed by heavenly star-status. I meet the English prophet John Daley, who produced the British master work *Hidden Agenda*, which was awarded the jury prize. Daley, the most daring and revolutionary of all the prophets with his brand of hell-fire Calvanistic diatribe. 'There's a lotta talent abaht,' he says in his shrewd South-London-Cockney-no-nonsense-breezy-at-South-end banter as he eyes the mini-skirted starlets who swim up to him like baby sharks wanting to feast on succulent producer flesh. He produced *Salvador*, one of the most blistering anti-war films of all time, when no one would go near it, and *Platoon* for a PS. He says he took twenty million dollars in sales and pre-sales this week and buys me a steaming cup of frothing cappuccino and we talk about the future where maybe a Berkoff film will be the new object of worship. I sit and smilingly reflect on my pilgrimage here.

FLASHBACK: A CROWDED HEATHROW AIRPORT. INTERIOR SHOT. *Pan on sweaty actor making his way to Gate 28. Shoulder bags cutting into his Armani shoulder pads. He arrives at the Departure Lounge. Long shot. A voice cries out his name.* Steven!!! Berkoff!!! *Fast close-up on actor's face. Panic registers at his name being so imperiously shrieked. Face recomposes. Cut to woman sitting with younger man, who looks comfortably protected by the older woman. It's an agent and her client! In fact the celebrated and distinguished agent Marina Martin! And her client Paul McCann!*

BERKOFF: Going to Cannes?

MARTIN: Yes, Paul's in a film. (*Close up her mouth – a trifle pouting with satisfaction*)

BERKOFF: OOOOOOOOOOoooooh, how wonderful! (*Close up his eyes – a trifle pinched with jealousy*)
Berkoff's eyes swivel round to McCann. Close up McCann, who seems dreaming of distant shores and wondering what I'm doing there. We face each other.

MARTIN: Saw your article in the *Guardian* this morning [May 19th]. I'm sure you'll get better service in Cannes!! Hah hah!!

BERKOFF (*surprised*): You read it? What a lovely way to start your morning, see ya . . .
The actor turns with a swift flick of the heel. The camera tracks his walk.

BERKOFF (*V.O.*): Silly Distinguished Agent!! My article was a metaphor for London and not my distress about getting service. I bet they're travelling Club Class, the swine, so I had better get on the plane before they see me going Economy because *I'm* paying my own bloody fare.
Berkoff mounts, steps into plane. Cut to interior. A yuppie couple are seated and the male is spreading his paper outwards and inches over to Berkoff's area.

Close up: Berkoff's eyes ricochet around his sockets and give occasional side-long glances as he tries to read the yuppie's paper.

BERKOFF: Look, do you mind folding your paper, then you don't have to shove your hand in my face.

Massive close-up as yuppie's eyes distend. Silence. Count five.

YUPPIE: Relax . . .

BERKOFF: I know there's not much space but use your intelligence!!

Close up yuppie, who says nothing.

YUPPIE (*V.O.*): What an asshole. I think it's that madman who plays madmen in movies.

BERKOFF (*V.O.*): Phew, I'm glad I did that, I feel better . . . these people get away with murder! I bet McCann's got a hotel fixed up. Five-star. Anyway, here comes the grub . . . *End of trailer*.

So, as I sit with John Daley, these little whimpering thoughts compare pleasantly with my present luxurious surroundings, and as I look into the crisp yellow laundered air of the Côte d'Azure, it is with utter delight that I see enough planes to mount a D-Day invasion slowly fly across my vision, and attached to these planes long pennants advertising that:

SUPERMAN 3 IS COMING BY ALEXANDER SALKIN

A panorama of flags strewn across the celestial sky with no fewer than twenty-six planes!!

Ah, I sigh, I am so lucky, to be truly in the centre of Mecca where miracles are thrown across the sky advertising the annunciation of 'SUPERMAN'! I nearly doubted coming here and might have stayed in the grim chilly climes and seen *The Wild Duck* or *The Krays* film again and bathed in myself immortalized in a dazzling performance and be accused of over-acting when really I was UNDER-ACTING!! However, now I am ensconced in the Carlton Terrace where the mob meet, which is like the wailing wall of the Carlton Hotel. Here scores of enthusiastic worshippers debate the Talmud of film law. Let there be film and lo and behold, bankers and money lenders sat giving out benedictions, and busy tanned men with gaunt film faces went from table to table kneeling here and there and adopting those crouching positions so beloved of those who are used to getting hand-outs. The news is that *Cyrano* has scored the most points so far, *Wild at Heart* coming up on the outside . . . ah, Rupert Everett can be seen rushing up and down the corridors with his cap skew-whiff in the style of a Californian breakdancer . . . he looks busy and bustles down to the terrace where he settles and becomes another of the multi-headed magnitude which is now moving like sea anemones. I greet Christopher Walken whom I vaguely directed in *Coriolanus* and he is looking like a sleek cat and smiling with the unalloyed joy of one who suspects that this is better than the siren-screeching streets of Manhattan, and the only shrieks in Cannes are those that rise from the throats of sweet sirens with pursed cupid-lips, who sit adoringly with hairy-chested producers who in the animal kingdom wouldn't stand a chance in hell of a female animal of that sleekness to mate with his fat, tired old carcass. Laura Hutton just strolls in gleaming as if lights were installed behind her eyes. Meanwhile, between the tables slinks a photographer who suddenly freezes like a praying mantis and points his protuberance on a young cherub. The sacrificial offering sits lip-glossed and terribly self-conscious at the gross erection of a 200 mm. lens pointing at her like some satyr in the throes of satyriasis . . . he is waiting for the moment when self-consciousness will burst and her face will dissolve into a cappuccino of smiles. He stands, I swear, for five minutes without moving, like a rock lizard. The tension is extreme. His lens is a net scouring the bay for exotic creatures. I order tea with lemon and the drone of prayers continues around me: points, projects, deals, completion and 'How much for Canada? Three million? They must be crazy, I paid only six million for the whole of America!' I am alone now and isolated while the world teems around me, all knowing the language, the prayers and the rituals. I MUST GET SOMETHING TO READ! Ah, I spy in the foyer

Screen International, the whopper four-dollar version, so I snatch it off the table and take the sweetness of the Bible in my hands and it feels so good. I have in my hands the scroll more secret and more mysterious than the Dead Sea Scrolls. The oracle of the deities. The word of the gods. I read its single columns of poetry . . .

ALL-TIME FILM RENTAL CHAMPS, BY DECADE

E.T. USA 1981. SPIELBERG. $228 MILLION.

Ah, such bliss . . . now I am part of Cannes!

Second Avenue . . . Welcome to America . . . 1988

I stayed at the Gramercy Park Hotel in 3rd Street and Lexington. It was a marvellously old-fashioned establishment and not far to walk to the Public Theater in LaFayette, which is near the Village and close to Second Avenue, a slightly seedier avenue but full of fascination for the intrepid explorer. I would sit after one of my long journeys in one of the multitude of diners that line each avenue and record the thoughts of the day. Breakfast was the best time for my journal because American breakfasts are heavy food. The diners usually have high-backed cubicles and sizeable tables. Perfect for writing, drinking coffee and reading the daily news, the horrors of New York. And there are horrors!

A wheelchair in Second Avenue. An old man wheels his mobile steel home; on the back of his chair is attached a pouch for shopping. A bottle of mayonnaise peeks out of the whole mess. His grim unshaved face, his white-knuckled grip as he bends against the cold wind in Second Avenue, is a portrait of a grim struggle he must conduct daily. Somehow the portrait is softened by the bottle of mayo. He stops at a bus station. And the miracle. A silver bullet of a bus stops where the man and one or two others are patiently waiting. A hydraulic step that has been put there solely for wheelchairs slides down. He wheels himself on and the step lifts him up and on to the bus. The needs of the people . . . and there are a lot of people in wheelchairs in New York, more than I have ever seen in London. But then public pain is more common here. At least, you see more of it. Medical care costs. Hospitals and homes for the sick, aged and mental have been cut back by the right-wing Reaganites since he needed cash for the Contras. The crime rate here is on a level that is surreal (and what one reads is only the tip of the iceberg). Like all simple-minded people, the Reaganites or Thatcherites call for harsh measures without once addressing the root cause of crime, since they are conditioned to inflict punishment and violent revenge without considering the analysis of the problem. Analysis of the motives for crime smacks of liberalism and defuses the clout of immediate response which makes the punisher seem stalwart and strong, even Christian by the standards of today's Americans. So Bush calls for capital punishment for the murderers of two cops shot dead in one day in two different incidents, without even breathing a word about gun control. A gun killed. Guns have been ridiculously easy to buy since Bush feels that guns are necessary to uphold the Constitution fabric, apart from the fact that he is a card-carrying member of the National Rifle Association. People have stickers in the cars with the words 'TAKE MY WIFE, HOUSE,

BUT DON'T DARE TAKE MY GUN!' Guns are the obsession of a paranoid society and so Bush, and Reagan before him, will ensure that more cops will have large funerals like the one here recently attended by thousands of the boys in blue. Technically, theoretically, and even more, morally, you could accuse the Reaganites of being accessories to the crime by supplying the guns.

A man blows himself up in the subway with a home-made device strapped to his body. He rubs two pieces of tinfoil together to set it off. Imagine what goes on in such a mind, that can assemble a complex detonating machine but in his need for human contact elects to commit hara-kiri in the public subway. His familiar terrain. And what could be more horrific than the story of a chauffeur from Israel who came to the land of plenty eight years ago. Married, with two beautiful children waiting at home, he is stabbed and then finished off by strangulation with a shoelace. The killers take the dead man's house keys. Somehow they find his address and give it to their cronies as a perk since the house will now be without its protector . . . *five* men go to the house where by now his family anxiously wait. The men wear Halloween fright masks. They handcuff the wife to the bed and proceed to rape her and her sixteen-year-old daughter. Not yet quite content they slash them with knives and attack the daughter with a broomstick. Welcome to America. The disquieting fact is that these horrendous crimes are not the bizarre act of a lone mind-rotted assassin but of organized gangs working in large groups. Thus the conclusions can only be drawn that the system of ruthless and free competition, with little provision made for the ones that fall by the wayside, produces sick monsters. What a stockpile of murdering and raping barbarians is now being produced and nurtured in the bleak heartlands of the Bronx. I walk to work past numerous upturned palms begging for 'a little change' . . . the sights are loathsome: a battered face stares out of a ragged old coat, shivering on the pavements are down-

and-out street-vendors selling mouldy old editions of *Vogue* or second-hand books. Elton John played at Madison Square Garden last night and the papers are full of the billionaire's wife, Mrs Donald Trump, with her teeth hanging out in hysterical excitement, along with other wildly grinning celebs, while a few blocks away . . .

Concorde . . . 1989

I had to do it once, the ultimate trip. It was even more than I imagined and I felt like a tiny insect on a leaf being slowly wafted along the breeze. Coriolanus *had opened in New York to very good reviews and now Baryshnikov was about to open in my American première of* Metamorphosis. *I decided to treat myself.*

This is sheer wonder . . . a kid's fantasy . . . a supreme and ridiculous idyll . . . a mesmeric onslaught of the senses. We're flying at sixty thousand feet; ten miles in the air . . . almost in space . . . the surge of power pulses through the engine as millions of volts smash into life. You step into another world . . . the cool world of money. At Kennedy Airport, as the porter gladly takes your bag, you might be stepping into a five-star hotel . . . no more the draggy queue as you push your cases inch by weary inch to the check-in counter. Here all is serene as you step into the pampered luxury of the rich . . . no madding crowd and just a handful of passengers at the desk . . . the world is calm here, you get the impression that only you are travelling as your boarding card invites you into the Concorde Club, the inner sanctum where you enter a space of cool grey silences. A peace closes over your raddled New York head. Your brain pitted with shrieks of sirens from the perpetual wounded beast of a city . . . your tongue coated with the food of a hundred lands. So leaving the towering turrets whose peaks stab the cloud, leaving the broken and pot-holed avenues, leaving the twenty-four hour life and endless liturgy of death in our daily news, leaving the daily breakfast from my local deli delivered to your door. Leaving its teeming uncensored streets that cascade with the supreme follies of life. Leaving its gargantuan avenues that disappear into the horizon like an Amazon of concrete and steel, I step into the hushed grey lounge which is really a sedate sound-proof club surrounding a fount of goodies displaying itself in the centre of the room . . . a stewardess gently suggests coffee and croissants.

You slip your shoulder-aching hand luggage into a shelf, grab a paper from the vast selection of British news whose very variety demonstrates the variegated phenomenon of British thinking, and not the one quality and two tabloids available for ten million people in New York. Here, laid out, is a welcoming glut of papers, a flag of opposing thoughts and style and ways of thinking, the *Guardian*, *The Times* and the *Independent*, the leading trio. Not clothed like their New York counterparts with the ads after page two and then having the effrontery to call itself a newspaper while the giant underwear display shoves the single and forlorn news column right to the edge of the bed.

From the lounge Concorde could be seen, beaky and waiting and looking astonishingly smaller than it does from the air, its wings seeming almost to have retracted. I sat in a grey sofa opposite some men in grey who talked in grating, over-hearty voices which caused me to shift, dragging my tiny breakfast bagel with me, since their crude tones were not in keeping with this brave new world.

The Concorde waiting below was like a great swan at its mooring. The advantages of wealth are hygiene and precision, and how pleasant to be treated to clean cold steel, small delicate cups and a permanent fountain of coffee . . . cute miniature bagels, all things which are not in themselves expensive. It is curious how the poor and working-class in Britain feel safe in places that are down-trodden and wretched when it's cheap to have things that are clean, fresh and inventive. So I sat in sheer disbelief, returning to a state akin to childhood, about to embark on a journey on the greatest toy on earth. Next to my soft grey sofa was a phone. I could call anyone in New York and still drink my coffee from my demi-tasse, chew my mini-bagel and keep one eye on the *Guardian*. I finished the coffee and returned for a refill. Champagne bottles stood rigidly to attention – their mouths unstopped and willing, and all, naturally, free – although you have paid ten times the cost of an economy flight to be able to be cocooned in luxury for three hours forty minutes over three thousand miles of sea.

So I sat and waited in the tranquil grey zone and recalled the Manhattan days . . . the hotel room at Gramercy Park swiftly vacated at 7.30 a.m. . . . the luggage of a five-month stay . . . the memories of the view outside the window of the little park in full autumnal splendour and then stripped down to its raw branches and lined with snow, and then warm again as I watched the seasons change through that square of window in Room 920. The last look at Gramercy Park under a grey and damp New York day. I saw my play the night before and the whole house bravo'd.

At last we enter our metal bird. The business men are scanning the market. 'MONEY', 'AMEX ISSUES', 'CHANGE UP', 'CHANGE DOWN', 'VOLUME COMPARISON', squeal the leaders as we are about to pierce the skies at the speed of a bullet. Concorde is a formidable work of art, the utter supreme agony of creation wedded to science and welded to fantasy, a plane shaped like a bird, the curved neck of a white swan. A polymorphous mix of esoteric alloys whose cells have gripped and bonded for ever with the whirling nuclei, a metal blend unlike any other.

We're off! And before long the mighty javelin seems to be skimming the stratosphere . . . a green sign appears on the wall (height 52,000 ft, m.p.h. 1340! temp. -59c). All this as we sup on Cuvée Dom Pérignon 1980 and feast on appetizers. A selection of canapés: caviare, salmon and citrus fruit laid out like a flower. A menu is thrust into your hand, its white pristine shape chilled as if written contents were as perishable as the actual. The serviette wrapping the silverware is also chilled where it has rested in the icy regions of space. I unfold the precious instruments; we're still climbing until we reach sixty thousand feet and I can almost see the earth's curve.

How slowly we climb now, where the air has little substance for the plane to grip, even though we've increased speed to 1350 while I finish the hors-d'oeuvre and read about the Harrods fraud or dubious take-overs and British life unfolds like a tacky soap opera. Will the scheming Lonhro defeat the plotting nefarious Arab! (This is the *Observer*'s scoop – the dreary contortions of the filthy rich and greedy who wish to embrace that lovely dowager of England, Harrods.) The grey men are still reading, heads buried in the pink pages of the *Financial Times*.

I meanwhile lift my head from my Pérignon, my canapés, my caviare, my chilled cutlery, my poached salmon, and survey through the small eye of the porthole endless space. A piercingly bright blue sky is draining its rich cobalt to the earth. There were clouds over New York when we accelerated into space, leaving them behind, impaled on a crown of spires. We break through the cloud with never a tremble, unlike those who associate with fat sturgeon-like jets whose every tremor has you praying. This penetrating silver fish shot through and up into the perfect blue world, bright, scintillating, sharp and pretty.

The clouds that were like mashed potatoes now have developed some curls and the stewardess offers more champagne. Everything is perfect, even the pull-out table is finely joined and welded with thin metal hinges and my fruit salad is devoured . . . the cold cooked salmon I guiltily picked at since I didn't need it . . . I feel the engine's power coursing through the plane and under my feet, its energy awesome as with its swept back delta wings and curved beak it impersonates a giant eagle and tears through the sky, which now deepens to the blue you see through broken glass, that pure intense blue when light is fractured and reveals its naked core, that deep, almost purple blue. The clouds now have developed some form and the wall sign reads 54,000 ft up . . . the captain's voice assures us that we are now only a hundred and twenty miles from Ireland and yet so far up we seem to drift slowly through space at 1350 m.p.h. It's -52 degrees outside as we float through an inferno of icy blasts in the airless void. In here we are almost too warm, in the belly of this slim silver bird that nourishes us on sherry or cognac. There is a slight braking and I feel myself go forward as we lop off a hundred miles an hour . . . and now we're really losing speed and another hundred miles vanishes in less than a minute. I can even feel the difference as we lope along at a modest 1000 m.p.h. I've eaten and drunk and written for a couple of hours and now we're approaching Ireland at 55,000 ft where the sky is empty of anything but us and I see from the writing on the wall that we're dropping and again I feel myself go forward. Lost 5000 ft, 12.32 p.m., 870 m.p.h., we expect to arrive slightly ahead of schedule, three and a half hours!

For a moment we came within sight of heaven, and it was the colour of the sea when the sun is slanting away, a rich and deep marine blue, so luminous, so perfect, so clean, and now we slowly descend into the grey soggy wet clouds of England.

Two hundred and seventy miles to go and 630 m.p.h. I like to feel part of the process, as if I were reading the dashboard on a car . . . it's very cloudy now but the temperature has risen dramatically to 9 degrees at 11,500 ft . . . I could be in Los Angeles now, walking in the sun . . . 12.57 p.m., 9000 ft at 330 m.p.h., a bit slow, and now I can see how slowly one can go . . . 1.01 p.m., 7000 ft and seventy miles to go . . . 310 m.p.h. A voice behind me echoes my thoughts . . . *'How slow can this thing go?'* . . . but he adds my unspoken thoughts . . . *'before it drops out of the sky?'* . . . Suddenly the countdown on the wall of the cabin stops. A sign comes up in its place. 'THANK YOU FOR FLYING CONCORDE'. Obviously they don't want us to start getting funny ideas. It was a great flight.

The Evil Regime . . . Reagan . . . Gramercy Park . . . 1989

Of course my morning breakfast stints in a small café off Third Avenue had me verbally regurgitating all that I had absorbed, and after a while the American obsession for gratification became too much. Sometimes it seemed like a giant mouth – a Rabelaisian monster that would never be satisfied no matter how much you fed it.

An old bent-backed chappie crawls down the square, so old and decrepit that but for his enormous wealth he would have been pushing up daisies long ago. A wind nearly lifts him around the corner into Third Avenue, where I pick up the national paper, *USA Today*, a well-tailored semi-tabloid which seems permutated to cater to the variety of tastes of Middle America. It's slim and divided by four. The four sections of the American wheel of life. According to the book *The Seven Arrows*, the Indian medicine wheel resembles the spokes of a bicycle wheel where each stands for a different attribute of human content and all make up the whole in order to be in a state of harmony. Thus you should have the qualities of the eagle in daring and in vision but also the timidity and humility of the mouse, courage but not fecklessness, and so according to the Red Indian each point in the compass must balance with another, be both bear and cat, since all parts make up the world and give it balance and, as we know, an unequal emphasis in one creates disorder in another. *USA Today* is the American wheel, catering for the reduced four needs that feed its readers: news, sport, money, life. The 'life' section has a lot to do with TV ratings, Liz Taylor, Donald Trump and other mediocrities whose celebrity status has much to do with collecting money and self-obsession. Cher, an ex-singer turned actress famed for her wooden expression, is seen on TV extolling the virtues of mindless exercise of the body while the mind vegetates in a garbage heap of moribundity and primal needs. The front page of the 'life' section gives the latest movie grosses, since movies and what they gross are now an obsession, no longer an art form or means of a higher form of communicating the ills of America or even a vehicle for illuminating entertainment. In the obsessive sports-mad culture movies score points like football. One film noses ahead, like horse-racing, the stars might be football players. Then some flak on AIDS which is an excuse for another ongoing soap, with rating and deaths reported almost weekly, new cures, charity bashes given for the rich and famous and a reason to get out the house without feeling guilty about a splurge. Score count: 48,000 deaths and mounting. Soon exceeding the Vietnam death roll. Eddie Murphy is reported as being 'still hot' and the new mini-series *Lonesome Dove* scores 37 per cent of the viewers, out-running *Six Tapes* . . . *Lonesome Dove* stars Robert Duvall and Anjelica Huston, who are photographed wearing ten-gallon hats and riding horses. Hats seem to imply some kind of cultural integrity and impose 'character' on a void. Not that Duvall is a void, he is a skilled actor who exudes high moral tone, although at fifty-eight he talks about his 'girlfriend', which is charming and shows that you don't have to age gracefully in the land of the ever-young where youth and virility is the holy grail. Now everybody has girlfriends, not friends, women friends, companions or ladies, but 'girlfriends', a kind of gelatinous term I was reluctant to use as a teenager.

Yes, there's even a tad about the theatre and about Brit plays like *Pravda* by David Hare which is considered 'too heavy' for Broadway but may get a run in at the Guthrie Theater in the provinces. Its director uses the baby talk so much in vogue here . . . 'It's scary to do a play that is so vitriolic about the press' . . . I hear that President Bush used this retarded term so beloved of teeny-boppers at a horror-shlock film . . . its use implies a maudlin desire to be thought of as 'human' or 'vulnerable' . . . 'Gee, it's scary to be in the White House'. Apart from kindergarten words, two other words currently in vogue are 'exponential', a mathematical term used to describe everything from the Amazonian rain forest being destroyed to the increase in carbon in the atmosphere, and oxymoron, which seems to denote a sentence containing opposite and conflicting meanings, e.g. Reagan's 'compassionate' view of the homeless and unemployed. Not much else apart from TV ratings in the mini-series, and after four pages for the 'real world' we have no fewer than eight pages for sport, and Mike Tyson's divorce from Robin Givens has involved the nation's brains for three months. We have had a blow by blow account of another soap horror of the child murder in which Joel Steinberg, a New York middle-class yuppie, habitually beat his adopted child over a period of a year until at last the poor creature succumbed to his abuse. His badly mauled wife, who now looks like an ex-boxer, was given immunity for testifying against her torturer. This story gripped New York by the short and curlies for months as the loathsome testimony leaked out like a suppurating wound day by day into the avidly read tabloids. Topping this story, or taking the limelight as it were, was a lunatic gunman firing an automatic AK 47 at school kids, and while Washington has the highest per capita murder rate in the USA, of which 60 per cent are drugs-related, it seems impossible to control the sale of guns, so despite stringent laws on drugs as well as swimming topless anyone can still buy these weapons of destruction and national havoc since they have been enshrined in the Constitution, and are as much a totem as religious relics. Kids take guns to school, so easy is accessibility, and the 'Saturday night special' is a small hand-gun lethal enough to blow your brains out. That so many guns exist in a volatile nation of over-achievers whose brains have been zapped daily by a fusillade of commercials extolling the good life would seem to be asking for trouble, and it is, since kids regularly blow up their mums or teachers for some denial of their needs. Do not deny the needs of greedy achievers who are armed, even if they want your sports shoes, since they will kill you for it. The other big news, apart from the monotonous braying of Liz Taylor and Trump, is crack. Kids out there are trafficking vials at five dollars and earning hundreds of bucks a day. Try stopping that! It's all part of free enterprise and demonstrates a grittiness on behalf of the kids to compete with the system which preaches daily that if there's a market and a need, go for it.

It's a free enterprise system, after all, and if you fall down nobody picks you up, and if you are black, unemployed and sick then see how the state helps you when you have offered your life for them in Vietnam. See how long you have to queue in disgusting overcrowded corridors in charity hospitals because of your government's obsession with the dangers of socialism. So crack is the natural result. It may provide an insurance, since doctors and surgeons in America view your body as their treasure chest and thousands of operations are performed on women who don't need them, and the surgeons are starting to resemble Burke and Hare, the body snatchers, as they persuade women to have their uterus removed after the age of thirty!! Or if they have already had children. The results now discovered of this needless op are reduced sex drive and depression, since even in menopause hormones are still functioning. Vasectomies are also gratefully pounced on and breasts removed as opposed to merely removing lumps. Your body is a gold mine, so beware the kindly advice of your doctor: I would be very wary of a doctor who viewed me as frozen assets.

The Run . . . Venice, LA . . . 1989

I always enjoyed my stays in LA and found a sanctuary in a motel at the end of Venice beach. Venice was made up originally of canals after dragging the mosquito-infested swamps, and so it was called Venice. It was a beautiful and charming resort at the beginning of the century but suffered neglect and decay in the fifties – to be resuscitated in the seventies and eighties. Venice fascinated me when I first discovered it and was my intro to California. I live there every time I go back and it has become my American home. I wouldn't think of living anywhere else and if any place had a spiritual affinity for me it was here. Of course, others have felt that too, including Jack Kerouac, Gregory Corso, Charlie Chaplin and even Charles Manson.

Delicious day but crowds starting to move in the sidewalk café since I'm here later than usual . . . 11 a.m. and the place is packed . . . ran almost all the way to the public open-air beach gym and felt splendid . . . felt marvellous. Ran like an old aching man at first, with supreme effort dragging one foot ahead of the other.

Before my run I stop for 35 cent coffee at Tom's Café where the relics of civilization sit and eat their eggs off paper plates. I stare out of the window while a woman with fat legs and heavy shoulders tattooed on one side attacks the video machine. The oriental lady serves me with a tranquillity that has somehow been preserved in the cess-pit of Tom's Café, and so I drink my 35 cent coffee and survey the boardwalk . . . a few faces are out, and there is quite a bit of pre-work activity. It is 7.30 a.m. already . . . I pace myself, walking for a moment to drink my coffee and survey my life on this morning.

The sky is eggshell blue and scattered with white silk plumes. The air is silk and I attempt to hoist one knee up only to feel it crash down to earth again. Try to feed some bolts of lightning into those pneumatic joints, and eventually find I am running and jogging and I know it's only till I reach the Pritkin Institute, that gaunt building where armies of the overweight can be seen through the windows, walking endlessly on their treadmills like condemned rats. I will then stroll the last fifty yards to the outdoor gym. I trickle past the sidewalk café not open until 9 a.m. in the winter months; a lone wetback cleans and prepares the tables. [*As I sit and write this in the sidewalk café two guys are rapping the table demanding the check and Dianne from the bookshop says,* 'You still here,' *since this is where I sat last night*.]

So I run past the little synagogue on the boardwalk, a tacky little affair but always occupied and so perfectly part of the Venice strip and its cafés, boutiques, stalls selling everything from sunglasses to skateboards, second-hand leather boots, crystals to clear your brain-waves, pizzas and Polish dogs . . . run past 'TUUM EST', the drug rehabilitation centre, then past the Fig Tree Café where I have eaten many a spinach salad coated with warmed olive oil and where the smell of cinnamon cookies pervades the air. Past the apartment I once lived in with a courtyard where we picnicked at the wooden table one Sunday five or six years ago, and the same table has now collapsed but it is still chained by one wooden leg. I run past the poor refugees of Los Angeles who are gathered under a tree . . . a blanket stretched out bearing a few scraps to sell including an old dog-eared book, past an obese woman who sits with a man who seems to be her protector, although she appears wounded since a crude piece of plaster covers an area where once a seeing eye lay comfortably ensconced.

Her plaster seems sucked into the space. I run past my past, through the wooden fences which define the territory I know as Venice . . . past the Jewish centre where the aged remnants of Europe congregate or sit on benches opposite, hanging on to the three-pronged walking sticks and topped with cotton baseball caps which somehow mock the inactive sack of bones beneath 'New York Yankees'. Past and onwards, past the pity of human life sleeping on the beach or on the benches, bodies twisted up like corkscrews as if enclosing themselves like leaves. Black, white, young, thin . . . 'Spare some change?' is the American song of the eighties.

But on and on, now I start to sense the first prickle of sweat dribble down and look to see that I have bashed ten minutes and the old pier at Santa Monica shimmers in the distance, delightfully glistens and seems to move in the morning haze, the shape growing larger by the stride . . . the giant wheel, the orange cupolas, the brown wooden stairs, the green roofs . . . blue misty hills of Topanga Canyon behind. I smash my old white Reeboks into the new asphalt where thin high-tech bikes whizz past in the bike lane opposite. The brown roof of the Pritkin Center gets larger . . . the hills seem to glow with a bluish tinge and are toothed with little white squares which in the distance carry mystery the way twinkling lights do across a bay at night . . . so mysterious and elusive . . . the run gets easier and my body undoes itself. The pores open, the doors release their grip and I flow inside my own gravy; pounding past the Pizza Hut, still closed, but under whose canopy lie the sleeping dead . . . dead to the world, lying on rags or even sleeping bags, some old sheets, a group of maybe three or four, a little sanctuary, and next to the sleeping head of one lay a book, something to cling to so that there may be life after death, some structure, not just sit all day, wander up and wander down, small talk on the seats, the small snaky chat to deflect the pointlessness of just sitting, scoring some loose change. Past them and on to the final stretch, and on my left the thin blue scarf of sea meets the blue canopy streaked with white wispy moustaches, and on and past the apartments of smart Santa Monica on my right, white stone and concrete igloos, carefully lawned public places and wooden picnic tables, past the public toilets where if it's cold the refugees sleep for the night. Past an old man screaming at his wife . . . *'Of course I don't hate you . . . If I did I'd tell you . . . I'm not a Jew or black . . .'* and on and on and it's fifteen minutes and the skaters whizz past in droves like angry hornets on these new skates which are two single wheels, not balanced, more like ice skates; then a woman skates past with a dog in tow followed by a man with a dog in tow, then two skaters shoot past, one's head facing the other's arse, in perfect unison, the one in front like a mirror for the one behind, cutting the air, streamlining themselves, their arms slashing the air like scythes, and still on and on and nearly there, the sky, sea, air and distant hills with white teeth-like outgrowths getting marginally bigger, the pier growing larger and Malibu looking inviting and reeking of perpetual summer and I'm nearly there . . . I'm heading round the corner to the Pritkin Institute and looking forward to seeing the disembodied heads bob up and down through the windows, I put on a spurt of speed, just a little teasing of the pistons, see how much lactic acid I can summon from the motors, see how the tendons will snap back, and now I'm slowing down . . . slowly ease up and stop, slowly go into a walk for the last fifty paces. It feels wonderful to stop, and problems dissolve down my back as I stroll to the outdoor municipal gym. A few guys are already 'chinning' at the bar and working out in the morning heat . . . just quietly pulling their bodies up to the bar and dipping them between their shoulders on the parallel bars and looking much like those wooden puppets set between two sticks that leap round and round.

The Barrymore Theatre . . . New York . . . 1989

After directing Roman Polanski in Paris in my stage version of
Metamorphosis *I was asked to do it in New York with*
Baryshnikov – I was very excited to be directing an artist of such
astounding calibre, and grateful to Roman Polanski since he
had persuaded Misha to take on the role after the Russian dancer
had seen the film director perform it in Paris. It was an odd play
to be doing amidst the crumbling old theatres of Broadway.
They made a sad and sorry sight as they slowly decayed.
Decayed from a lack of critical response, since with only one
major newspaper of quality there is little protection from
alternative critics against a bad review – plus the unbridled
demands of unions and the prohibitive costs. The great shame is
that New York was made for drama, but there is little
opportunity for it to surface. New York was once the home of the
greatest modern drama on earth.

Broadway seems a bit flaky, a desert waste set within a few diseased streets and backing on to Eighth Avenue where homo skinflicks vie with peepshows. This turns back on to the long meandering streets that head down to the river. It used to be called 'Hell's Kitchen', an area of tenements occupied by Irish and Italian immigrants, but now being slowly bulldozed while the yuppie kingdom spreads westward.

When a show dies a theatre stays empty and rotting until a new punter gives it life. It's not used, and the chances are that it won't be, given the present poverty of critical response, where one mousy reviewer can make or break a show, and only the crass and simple now survive, the unions and critics together seeming only to have produced unfortunate miscarriages. The owners are not inclined to give their theatre a lick of paint, since it could be dark for months . . . or years! The gangsters of real estate hang around like vultures waiting to pounce and get the steel ball swinging. If a theatre owner neglects his property he hopes the local council will condemn it and thus bag him a big killing. There is a beautiful old theatre called the Biltmore which has now been dark for years, standing empty and rotting as a testament to market values applied to culture. There was even a rumour that the owners are vandalizing it by leaving doors and windows open to accelerate the process of decay.

The Barrymore, where we open *Metamorphosis*, is being given a tiny face-lift, a little powder and paint here and there for her firstnight party, when Nancy Reagan among others will be decorating the stalls. The acrid fumes of the operation permeate the passageway into the stage door. The Barrymore is newer than most, dating from the twenties, and is still in its prime. It's a beautiful building designed in the Edwardian/Victorian style and with only one balcony. The Shuberts, a famous theatrical dynasty, own this among a dozen others while the other empire, the Nederlanders, own the rest.

The theatres are more like mausoleums for a dying art form, great old sailing ships from a bygone age, fading and peeling gently while the fear of the fate of the Biltmore, the terror of being dark and sterile like a cold gaunt widow, tempts owners to stay wedded to the same production for years. Long after its creators have lain in the earth they will be represented by a group of dancers kicking their legs for the ten thousandth time. *Cats* inevitably rolls on for all from Middle America whose only excitement is the fact that it is 'real', compared to their plasticized, synthetic and media 'reality'. The haunted heartlands of American TV where the commercial is the mantra of civilized life and where everybody speaks in the disembodied joy-speak of the jingle.

Even *Oh! Calcutta!*, Ken Tynan's brave fantasy and taboo-breaker, has gradually wilted into old age and senility. It was meant to shock and expose hypocrisy but now mocks the liberated period that spawned it.

The dark widows wait to be claimed whilst they stand forlorn, being spat against, pissed on and assaulted until one day a show attempts to bring some fresh life into the womb once again. The old lady wears fresh paint and disinfects herself. The lights burn bright and the wardrobe department sets up shop. Cards are written with the actors' names on and affixed to the dressing rooms. The higher you go the smaller the role. A 'green room' has a permanent nipple of coffee on the go. The dressing-rooms are old and uncharitable but the actors make it a home while they stare in the mirror awaiting their call. A make-up box, a towel, some first-night congratulations to 'go out and get them', and while some rooms are laid out like a surgeon's operating table with paintbrushes soaking in spirit and make-up sticks lined up like instruments of battle, others like mine reveal a single squashed stick of make-up like a mangled tube of toothpaste, a couple of brushes and a roll of tobacco. The cards are laid out, since they are your support system, your flag of popularity that you contemplate as you sit in your cubicle and feel a distinct stirring in your bowels as the tannoy announces 'Half an hour, please.'

So we're on Broadway at last, at the Ethel Barrymore Theater which opened in 1928. Laurence Olivier passed through these portals in *No Time for Comedy* . . . Brando spent a long season perfecting his acting style in *Street Car* and the stage-door man proudly shows me the basement where Brando fooled around between acts and had his nose broken, and who was understudying him . . . why, Jack Palance. So I walked the same steps as Brando as he turned down the passageway, and Deborah Kerr in *Tea and Sympathy*, Sidney Poitier, Henry Fonda, Michael Redgrave, Orson Welles in *Moby Dick* . . .

Next door to the Barrymore and rudely upstaging her are the jagged spikes of scaffolding from the building work which stops only for matinées, and then continues its machine-gun drills as soon as the audience pour out.

A couple of blocks down, the legendary Sardis was like a morgue, as if a plague had demolished only the theatre world. I went in to taste the flavour of success and found it empty. The menu was for fast-food tourists and while the cartoons of the great and famous littered the walls, the tourists dining beneath distinguished noses ordered steaks and scampis. I had actually phoned to book a table for Saturday night at 8 p.m., wishing to impress a very special woman whose fame and talent lit up a small corner of my world. I entered the great Sardis to find about six couples eating disconsolately.

The customers pour in after *Lend me a Tenor* and another Neil Simon. Our show is the talk of the town, or the 'Street', as they call it. 'The word on the street is that the "lighting" is up for a Tony,' said the lighting man to me in the bar opposite the theatre where we were watching the stretch limos discharge their lacquered occupants on their way to see *Mischa*.

Sometimes before the show I like to stop at a deserted deli further down the street, where I consume the most fantastic chicken soup and matzo balls. 'You Steve?' . . . 'Yeah, that's right' . . . 'Listen, come by for a glass of champagne after the show, break a leg' . . . I leave the café, the Gaiety Deli, weighed down with the matzo balls, and dive into the maelstrom of noise as the drills and steel bits get a hard-on as they rape and destroy a whole area. A dozen new blocks are going up around 42nd Street. The theatres sit and wait for the death sentence, some dusty and bereft of fruit and some still proclaiming their last wares, whose occupants and applause have long faded into the twilight zone, but as if ashamed they clothe themselves with the old posters, while ironically another hoarding on the same dark theatre announces . . . 'See a show on Broadway'. The crowds pour out and the limos slowly slide in to harbour in the side street.

Theatre is memory . . . 'Remember the time we saw Baryshnikov play a beetle?' . . . 'Yes, we saw him, actually saw him at the Barrymore' . . . a memory which is indelibly printed in the mind as something precious, since it cannot be re-examined like a film. In some way a performing artist's greatest gift is their mortality. It makes those moments in the theatre the most valued, since we have shared it with him or her on that night. The night we saw Baryshnikov, Brando, Olivier, José Ferrer, Henry Fonda, Orson Welles etc. etc.

Twenty Years of Metamorphosis . . . 1989

The culmination of this story. The incredible tale by Franz Kafka ends up on Broadway with a Russian dancer, the most famous on earth, an English director of Russian ancestry, produced by Lars Schmidt, a distinguished Swedish producer who lives in Paris and was the last husband of the late Ingrid Bergman – we rehearsed in a large studio near the Gramercy Park Hotel and I recall Mischa's desire for perfectionism extending from dance to drama – he was a very moving beetle.

Baryshnikov is OK. He strides in the rehearsal room looking like something out of *L'après-midi d'un faune*, crossed with a street urchin or wicked imp. Sometimes when I'm desperately trying (unsuccessfully) to direct one of the other actors, Mischa will just sit quietly in his beetle cage, legs stretched classically out, and patiently wait for his moment . . . and then I see the training of the classical dancer, the waiting while the choreographer sets in motion other corners of the canvas, waiting for his turn until he too is 'fitted' into place. Serene, unhurried. Actors tend to wait by reading newspapers or distracting themselves with small chat or even crossword puzzles since it helps relaxing until you're called. I tend to write when hanging about on the rare occasion I perform in TV. I recall one time taking out my notebook when sitting at a scene which was a conference table. The director was setting up the shots and no acting was needed but the presence of my notebook seemed to imply a great threat to the floor manager, who insisted I get rid of it. As if my words were something of a threat to the codswallop I was acting in.

Baryshnikov runs the American Ballet Theater with its fifteen million dollar budget. It is situated downstairs from where we rehearse, and so while taking on the role of Gregor Samsa, the famous beetle in my adaptation of Kafka's *Metamorphosis*, he is also bearing the full burden of his dance company and thus fulfils the lines in the play when Gregor the insect hero refers to his parents: 'their fortunes rest on my back like a great weight'. Apart from a strong accent and a natural disinclination to use words like 'the' or 'a' his athlete's body pours itself into the Gregor-mould and he transforms himself into the black oppressive bug, a twitching sub-human thing, his legs splay out behind him in a way that only a dancer's could and he moves in small segmented jerks. He likes to work and mine incessantly the same scene, with none of the weariness that is usual among actors who want to move on and let the details colour themselves in organically later. A dancer must already have it on the night. An actor will wait and afterwards see what 'happens' . . . this is Chris Walken's method. He likes to leave a scene rare to underdone and let it cook in front of the public who will inform him how they like it. He prepares in front of you. Baryshnikov is new to acting and like many dancers sees more in it than there is sometimes, although there can be a great deal to think about. That's if it doesn't come naturally. He is obsessed with the speaking of the lines and is getting them into his system. I feel a huge responsibility in guiding him over the uncharted waters of our profession and yet not wanting to get too precious about it. He listens intently and watches me with an eagle eye. I am aware that this is one of the greatest articulators of human flesh the world has, and he is concerned about a simple sentence.

The movement is better as he glides across the floor and I suggest and demo the mime of the beetle. Baryshnikov's voice is developing and getting stronger and he tells me his friends don't recognize him on the phone. So for once I am in the unusual position of teaching one of the world's great bodies how to move and, having shown him the blue-print, Baryshnikov takes it and shapes it to his own creation, advancing the idea to another level where every permutation of the armature of his body will be at service. He is redesigning the damned thing! Taking it to pieces and streamlining my old bug. It's still the old VW shape, round back, cross-armed and spread, crooked legs, that moves by capturing the rhythms of insect life . . . its sudden twists and freezes. Its seeming deadness and then frightening unpredictability.

Over the years actors have absorbed the role and added their own characteristics which have embedded themselves in the present one. From Asher Tsarfati in Israel came a crazy humour and farting from the over-stuffed bug . . . from London's Tim Roth came the vicious alien beetle and the wonderful lizard-like

backward walk used in this to frightening effect when Baryshnikov can now crawl faster than his father can catch him. From
Terry McGinity, the first beetle after me, I have retained the
soulfulness, or tried to, and always hear his voice when the beetle
screams for the apple to be taken out of his back where his father
had embedded it. From Baryshnikov come incredible extensions
as he flattens himself under the sofa like a cockroach under a
stone. Each actor on the way adding to and taking from. From
Düsseldorf came incredible and acrobatic daring, and Polanski
added his dollop which was a kind of simplicity and dignity. In
our early balmy days Roman would rush to rehearsal across the
traffic-choked Paris streets, phoning from the car that he was now
at rue St Denis and a few minutes from the rehearsal studio, then
he would rush in with briefcase and scarf flying, saying he felt
like a schoolboy again. After work we'd flop in the tiny café next
door with its zinc bar and friendly North African manager and
drink a red wine together before going home. I felt and smelt
French. Here we don't do that since we don't have that friendly
little bar next door. We rehearse at 890 Broadway in one of the
giant dance studios which litter the downtown area where the old
warehouses from 23rd Street down have been adapted into vast
caverns lined with pumping, leaping and gyrating torsos. Next
door to us Chris Reeves has abandoned his Superman costume to
rehearse *The Winter's Tale* for Joe. He's playing Polixenes – we
meet in the little canteen and for the first time I see Clark Kent,
who looks extraordinarily handsome and much slighter than his
film image. He seems almost delicate, with a bird-like bone
structure.

I crawl back to our studio and go over the parts with the actors,
who seem reluctant to absorb the play, or else they are concerned
about absorbing it and I am reading the wrong signals.

The play sounded very romantic and touching in French but it
also felt very strong and earnest in German and again powerful
and epic in Hebrew. So the theme of a great work naturally

adapts to any language, it's only junk that falls apart when subjected to the overseas crossing and the realignment into another tongue. Junk writing, like junk food, is concerned with the superficial and waste product of society. It is not hewn or grown from its core. Kafka touches all of us in some way and when read in English does not sound alien. It sounds right in any tongue since its theme is neglect and human suffering.

It is always ironic in showbiz that a young, rich, famous prince of New York should play the disgusting, oppressed, neurotic and despised Kafka-bug, but that is the nature of the interpretive arts and if two multi-millionaires can play two tramps in *Waiting for Godot*, and make it work, so can Mischa play out the allegory of self-loathing.

Twenty years ago in 1969 I finally was able to put on *Metamorphosis*, my first full-length play, at the Round House, Chalk Farm. We were booked in for a miserable three weeks, which would be a mere try-out today, and yet those three weeks were amongst the most unforgettable of my life and the most exhausting. I preceded the play with another Kafka adaptation called *In the Penal Colony*, which is a harrowing *tour de force* and made necessary by the brevity of *Metamorphosis* – in those days it lasted an hour and a quarter. Over the years it has gained weight and is now at our last run-through one hour and forty! July 1969 was baking hot and Living Theatre had just departed taking *Frankenstein* with them. George Hoskins, who was a great and vivid administrator welcomed us, and I borrowed £550 at an interest rate of 49 per cent since I knew that we would be able to pay it back within a month. I was burning with confidence, which evaporated a touch when the temperatures soared into the nineties, but Harold Hobson's review of me as Gregor Samsa, in which I was flatteringly compared to the effect Henry Irving had in *The Bells*, was all a young actor could possibly hope and pray for. I had also directed/written and, along with a loyal friend, the architect Martin Beaton who designed it, raised the money for the production. The box office jumped and the audience sat and sweltered with us and on the last packed week I was intensely proud of the achievement. Naturally this led to no work being offered by any company and I went back to hustling a living until I could do it again. Now it has come a long way, our beetle from Chalk Farm '69 to Broadway '89. The box office opened last week and after one giant page in the *New York Times* we took $300,000 in the first week.

I think this is a very good creative move for Baryshnikov, since he is a dramatic dancer and the role spans the difference between dance and drama. Mischa's deep blue eyes face an invisible audience as he intones the first lines and struggles with those silly words and it hurts him to have to clamber painfully over the rocks of language when he flies so effortlessly through space. It is when he wakes up as the beetle that his full magic will be revealed. His fingers, clawed like talons, slowly open like a speed-film of a flower uncurling, followed by his body which gradually unbunches like a chrysalis emerging in the morning sun. He lifts his head and discovers his black metallic shape, his trunk lifts itself higher until he is an incredible inhuman hairpin and says very quietly, 'What has happened to me?'

We will see when the play opens at the Barrymore in March 1989.

PS *We didn't have to wait long. It was butchered by the butchers of Broadway and what else would you expect?*

Chris Walken . . . Coriolanus . . . 1989

Chris Walken was given to me as Coriolanus by the late Joe Papp. I was happy to have directed under the Papp regime and for the reason that he gave you his support, heart and soul. He rang me, funnily enough, in Ireland where I had just directed Salome. *There was a review of* Salome *in the* New York Times *in an article about Irish theatre. He read it and, in the characteristic way of New Yorkers, he rang me. 'Do you want to direct* Coriolanus?' 'Sure, why not?'

The sun has just peeped out as I sit once again in one of my favourite seats in the Lyric Café facing Third Avenue on the corner of 22nd Street. Were ever numbers so evocative? Across the road a red-brick building faces me, a comfortable, comforting three-storey, necklaced with fire escapes and with the 'Lamarca' pasta store beneath. Next door is Cameo Cleaners. The buildings are the remains of the nineteenth-century New York and give me a feel of the past. An overhead railway used to run the length of Third and the sun seldom got past it. I usually eat toasted bagel with cream cheese with coffee. They don't have pumpernickel bagels which are my fave, just plain ones. There's more variety of bagels at Kinder's round the corner on Park Avenue but then I don't have the view.

The show was better last night as Chris attempts to inject some life into it and succeeds. I think I have seen through his act. It is of a man using the text to show off brilliantly or get off on it. So there will be areas of deadness when the lines are spewed out in any kind of order and then those sudden lunges when a large voice leaps out and you know he is at his favourite deli counter. Here is pastrami and pickles and plenty of mustard. Then a period of inconsequence when he strolls sniffing through the store and then, sudden, impromptu and eccentric intensity when he sees something he likes and grabs it with an emotional charge and wolfs it down ravenously. Walken is a highly intuitive feline actor and would rather be guided by instinct than by intellectual reasoning. In consequence there are some dead areas where a little intellectual light is needed, but instead they are delivered in an anguished whine, and lack the authority of opinion. His authoritative tone has menace and he turns into a street-corner barracker. The patrician becomes the pleb he condemns. He came on last night for his first speech and started really well – half-way through his speech he 'went' or 'dried' and started a section

AGAIN! Quickly and thankfully sensing his flaw he picked up at the deli counter and munched on the familiar . . . 'What's the matter', delivered in a raging 'What's the madder!!' as he lambasts the plebs, a useful signpost for his reeling senses which puts him back on track. He fortunately left out 'ba-boom' when he says to Titus . . . 'thou shalt see me once more strike at Tullus' face, [ba-boom] – ' the audience lap him up. Next scene we do on mimed horses and in rehearsal he did an impression of John Wayne riding a horse; well, I have seen Mike Caine's impression of John Wayne but not on a horse. However, he did the horse scene well and was focused, though he still insists on saying 'the gates are ope' like 'the deli's still open', but leaps into the act again when he commands his boys, 'those that are most willing', to go into the fray. A sudden crescendo galvanizes the troops, and he is in his element with the lads.

The rest of the act passes normally and uneventfully until he enters with the funny walk of the bully-boys, which is outrageous since he was impersonating a kind of military strut of the soldiers, but it came out almost by accident as a gang leader's pose, a kind of leaning from left to right like a ship on high seas, and reminded me strongly of the walks adopted by the 'shtarkers'* of Stamford Hill! The scene when he confronts the tribunes is his best. A street fight and a verbal punch-up. A setting in the street puts Chris in his element. Smartly togged in black, double-breasted suit, he makes backwards and forwards lunges . . . sudden whip-lash . . . 'no take more!' He slaps a convenient pillar with a resounding thwack and dives in, but is held back by the gang, whose little cautionary movements flutter like wings in front of him without quite touching, suggesting even more the danger that might be unleashed without their restraining gestures. The audience likes him . . . he inputs 'street shtick' everywhere . . . little eeehs! and aaahs! A hybrid Brando/Pacino/Walken . . . the New York street-

*Toughies.

wise guy and anti-hero. The audience giggle at Chris and like that Shakespeare should be grabbed by the scruff and dragged down Delancey Street, the home of delis and street graft spawning the small-time punk who becomes a parody of himself singing his ultra-limited vocabulary and body language and thus lionized and exalted in a thousand movies. The mug is now hero since he spits at the yuppies and the values 'decent' people hold dear. Chris uses little nods and winks to the tribunes to suggest we understand each other, like a minor mafia figure. The audience eats it up, since in each overweight bourgeois opportunist is a tiny 'hood' . . . The scenes with Mum are good, inflammable, and with Irene Worth's steely voice are held together in a strong mesh, although at times she can put me in mind of a stern lady magistrate at a juvenile court. Very correct and incorruptible. Chris goes for the gut of the scene by reflex action, no mystery here since the audience feeds off 'relationships' and so we hear . . . 'Motheeeer . . . I'm goieeeeng' like a naughty child chastized for not picking up the bagels at the corner deli . . . the heavy second syllable means 'OK already' . . . Coriolanus won't lick ass and gets the big boot out of Rome. In the farewell scene with the family, he adds a Neapolitan touch and we are in the land of Godfather. I did, in rehearsals, invoke the Italian image to put some pepperoni in the playing, which was a bit bland. Chris took to it like a duck to water, and though the rehearsals were funny some of it has stayed . . . 'what' becomes 'wad, wad, wad, I shall be loved when I am lacked.' Then he scores a bull since ironically the Italian feel pays off on the line when referring to Hercules . . . 'six of his labours you'd have done and saved your husband so much sweat'. Even the line sounds modern. The audience goes for it. It's a good laugh and Chris drives it home. He is an actor with an ear for the audience like you have a nose for the street, you sniff out the opportunities, a faint tickle or chuckle from misunderstood intent will have him buckling the line to fit the misconception. Actors are prone to doing this since it is the player's natural perversity to score a laugh and therefore earn the warmth of an audience who likes a touch of irony with their corned beef. Chris now openly courts laughs. It's seen as a virtue in the long, difficult plain of Shakespeare.

The play chunders on to the second act, and the powerfully played Aufidius by black emerging Othello Keith Davies greets Coriolanus when he decides to join the enemy. Menenius wishes to court Corio back to Rome and beg forgiveness for Rome's treatment of its hero. Here Chris gives the cold hard Mafia treatment . . . 'Away' . . . he stares at poor Menenius and gives him the thumbs down. It is underplaying with a vengeance and you have to be good at it because you can throw it away and the audience with it. But they seem to be attentive. Mum comes with the family (I cut the children out of the scene, not necessary for a poor child to hang around for twenty minutes to say one line) – this is one of the most famous scenes in Shakespeare when Volumnia begs her son to spare the country that spawned him and somehow symbolizes the state, and how can you turn down MA! The scene is performed by Irene with commitment and dedication but it is a trifle static at first, the only time a scene of mine has vaguely resembled those awful Shakespeare productions where the actors stand limply around looking earnest when someone speaks. Irene was quite decisive in the way she wanted to play it and there were many discussions backwards and forwards, and in the end I was all the more relieved there was no child hanging around. Eventually we reached a good compromise and the scene worked well, although I hated seeing Coriolanus' wife and her friend hanging about like they were waiting for a bus. Irene played the scene with clarity and it revealed itself as one of the great anti-war scenes in drama. At the end of a long tirade it is Chris's turn to respond. He says, 'Mother, what have you done?' He takes her hand . . . Chris as a tough street merchant eschews all that emotional gush and keeps his distance, and betrays the text in my opinion. 'The gods look down,' etc. . . . . the gods laugh at the volte-face of the hard man, Coriolanus, but here Chris holds back and does not dissolve in a welter of tears . . . 'make my eyes sweat' . . . and while he could hardly bring himself to touch Mum he paradoxically holds Aufidius as he tries to invoke his new partner's sympathy in his cause. Chris's reaction when he has to give anything but fire and ice is a trifle cardboard. Coriolanus in the main is volatile and smells of cordite, and that is where Chris scores and the audience can't take its eyes off him, which is after all the hallmark of great acting, but the giving might have redeemed the character and so in parts lacked roundness. The play winds up and Chris gets to 'cut me to pieces you Volsces', and when he wants to put it into top gear Chris stands with the best, but eight shows a week are hardly conducive to sustained playing let alone mental health.

On Saturday they perform two shows and one on Sundays at 3 p.m. I wouldn't wish it on a dog. You cannot play Shakespeare's huge roles on a production line. The critics have been in and the cast are more relaxed. I step backstage to view my American actors, who incidentally speak the lines with an alarming clarity. Chris says, 'It went well, I think.' He is flushed with relief. 'Yes!' I add. 'It may be the best one so far.' The actors are happy since they have two nights off. An extra one for Thanksgiving. It's been a good experience. *Coriolanus* in New York! Who'd have thought it?

Going to the Movies in Hollywood . . . 1990

Sometimes a painter will hit upon a weird subject for no other reason than it got stuck in his craw. A writer similarly. Anyway, I have a desire to reconstruct experience into prose as if I might then discover some profound thread that holds existence together. This is movie-going in Hollywood.

Sunday: a beautiful day to wake up in – a perfect blue day. Saw Georgia Brown last night, one of the powerhouse performers in the theatre today, who suffered two huge Broadway flops in two years – *The Threepenny Opera* with Sting and *Madame Rosa* directed by Hal Prince – but made up for some of it by loaning her formidable energy to my West End revival of *Greek*. We've been planning to see a movie for the last two months. 'Hey, Georgia, what movie do you want to see?' 'White Hunter, Black Heart.' 'Where's it on?' 'Don't know' 'Georgia, do you have a paper there?' 'I threw it away.' A pause. 'It's on in Santa Monica,' I add brightly, since that is near me. 'You'll have to get me, I've no car.' Pause. 'Look,' I add, 'to save me making four journeys, why don't you take a cab there and I'll drive you back?' 'Got no money, used all my money in cabs this week.' She wins, and I have a pleasant drive to her mansion in Beverly Hills and the dogs start yelping but we get in the car and head off to the Century City Center which is nearby, and is like a shopping mall with food, food, food leaping at you from every hole in the wall. Every square of space is dedicated to responding to your drooling fantasy, every kind of food, diners, snack bars, take-aways, Mexican, New York Deli (we opted for getting there early to savour it). The cafés were nearly all full and the eateries really were symbiotic with the movie house in the same building, and this represents a new way of eating since the café no longer has to serve the ethnic needs of the area. No need to go to China Town, Little Italy or Soho since it is now all under one roof. So we bought two tickets for *White Hunter, Black Heart*, which is the most puerile piece of drivel I have seen in years, where Clint (few words) Eastwood decides to play a born raconteur based on John Huston and for the first time in a respectable career looks, now he has to deal with articulate sentences, like a man who has just learned the language. Also his voice has none of the drive of the raconteur,

111

the relish, the bite which these talkers have, but Clint half whispered it and would have been overwhelmed by any other speaker in the room except, in this case, the others have no lines in which to do this, and so respectfully listen to the *bons mots* and choice stories coming across in inverted commas.

Before this event I ate a sandwich in the new deli experience and the half looked like the side of a cliff. I had to open it to remove half the contents so that I could slice my pickled dill cucumber and lay it across the top. I performed the operation but it was still too high and so I kept removing slices of turkey until I was able, full stretch and resembling a Munch painting, to stuff it in. Georgia had a tuna which, after attacking for some time, she gave up on and the plate looked even more full than it was when she received it.

The whole food hall, where people chose not to sit but to walk around with their food, was awash with enough polystyrene to destroy another mile or two of ozone in the atmosphere and nearly every human biped was walking attached to a polystyrene cup as if it were a life-support system or drip, without which they could not possibly walk or survive. Most natives here are now finding life quite painful in the raw, and that is just to walk without having, at hand's-reach, a cup, a Walkman round their ears and chewing gum in their mouths, and often all three at once. All senses must be stimulated or stuffed at all possible times.

So we entered the movie house and ignored the long counter that was selling all the popcorn, candy, hot dogs, cokes and sodas in case you might expire during the two hours or less of the film, and so you can fill your ears, eyes and mouth simultaneously and even have a surreptitious grope, as many seemed to be doing. We sat in a quiet area away from the androids so as to avoid, as far as possible, being annoyed by what was for them concomitant with film-watching, not wishing to be spoil-sports by wanting to see the film only. Unluckily, at the last minute three bipeds sat in front – OK, but then two sat right behind and both groups had naturally availed themselves of half-gallon cartons of popcorn and the sweet sticky odour of the corn wafted into my nostrils as their obsessive fingers scrambled around the shared tub. I gritted my teeth and watched the awful film and was grateful to some charging elephants whose trumpeting mercifully obliterated their scratching for a few blissful moments. After a while longer of gritted teeth it seemed to stop. Eureka, they had greedily finished it fast but, oh no . . . these morons behind me were now sucking on a straw like a mum's teat, and the tide of Coca-Cola was going down, leaving crumbling rocks of ice that would rattle on each suck. Film for me is fantasy, and letting yourself be drawn in, and releasing gradually your grip on reality, and when some idiot continually destroys the possibility of your entering the nirvana because of their own anal greed, I get plenty mad. I turned once or twice, hoping that my body movements would signal to these cretins that I could hear the movements of their oral mastur-bations, but it made no difference as they sprawled out, happy to defy and add to your annoyance. After a while of practising the lines in my head, I thought I would turn right around (if the rattling persisted) and ask the yob to kindly try and be quiet, since he was spoiling the film. After one more crunching of ice, I did turn, and saw more clearly the waxen spoiled face with a sickly grin smeared all over it, and I performed my rehearsed speech. He made no answer but the film was quiet after that. Maybe he had learned the lesson that other people exist, and if so, good. The film groaned to its hideous finale and seemed to be about strong Americans who loved Hemingway while loathing the Brits, whose faces all looked like potatoes and who had a penchant for kicking blacks.

The drama and the turkey sandwich had made me thirsty and so, before the end of the film, I went out and asked for a medium Coke. The attendant gave me a quart in a giant cup. I sat down and was extra careful not to let the ice rattle when I sucked the straw.

Greek . . . Théâtre de la Colline . . . 1990

Greek, *my oedipal modern rewrite, first surfaced in a little Croydon theatre and was mounted seriously at the old Half Moon Theatre where it perfectly fitted that ancient small synagogue off Leman Street, E1. As the crowds poured in I recalled my father's tailor's shop just fifty yards away.* Greek *seemed to want to stay alive and was still kicking when I revived it in 1988. It became an opera, originally commissioned by Hans Werner Henze, and then was translated into French. I think it is kicking still as it plays in Paris in its first revival.*

George Lavelli, the artistic director of the Théâtre de la Colline, invited me over for the last night of *Greek*, which had been awarded two 'Molière' awards, one for the acting and the other for the play. I was well chuffed. I stayed at the beautiful baroque Hôtel de Regina facing the Tuilerie Gardens and which overlooks the rue de Rivoli, and from my window I could look down into the small square in front of the hotel where stands a magnificent equestrian statue of Jeanne d'Arc.

There was a ceremony outside my room and some singing and as usual the malevolent-looking police buses in attendance nearby. It was Joan's birthday and they were laying wreaths which also gave the opportunity for the National Front to mask their fascist paranoid tendencies with the guise of national historical sentiment. A row of tricolours on six white masts fan like wagging tongues in the light summer breeze, and the sky is that perfect blue that is so alluring a backdrop against the white 'empire-style' buildings. Jewish cemeteries had been obscenely vandalized, as if the Jews hadn't suffered enough under the Vichy rule of French collaboration, and the police were on high alert. However, I was delighted that the most anti-fascist play in Paris at the moment had been voted by the people, and that is the audience, as the best play in Paris, even if this fact was ignored by the English press, and in Paris it was called *A la Grecque*, or *Greek* to you. I was more than happy that a top nationalized company had honoured me and the play with a good production and acting that was superb. It was the consummation of my work and a vindication of a play that had been less than always well received here. My plays here are usually put on by me, since few else apart from stalwart adventurers, idealistic youths, university drama groups or prisoners serving life seem to possess the necessary mania, passion or simple desire to perform them. However, when George Lavelli heard the translated play perfectly re-created by George Dyson and Antoinette Monod at a reading, since they tend to test many plays this way, he decided it 'spoke to him directly' . . .

That night I entered a theatre that was swarming with expectant faces and the kind of young but not gauche, and not debauched either, or entertainment hags, but a healthy-looking and alert audience that has come expecting something and somehow they know they will get it. I sat, and the lights went down, and I waited. I have never seen a play of mine performed before by others: I was just one of the audience. Music echoes through the auditorium, a young man enters and in a demonic and enthusiastic, almost kinetic, display performs the opening speech of 'Eddy'. His performance is electric and I have seen nothing to match it. It is a dazzling firework display. My text breathes easy under the explosive symphony of the French language, it has caught fire and blazes.

I hear the English thoughts and ideas and the language wraps itself around them and fuses, seems inseparable, bonded and seamless. The audience laughs frequently and in bursts like cannon shot. The actor, Richard Fontana, one of the best in France and a member of the Comédie Française, has been especially released for this role. He may not play in commercial theatres, only in state-run theatres that are not geared to commercial exploitation. He spits out Eddy's diatribe like grape pips; each word, syllable, consonant rendered perfectly clean as if he were savouring a feast. The French language has this elasticity, which actually suits *Greek*, and his delivery is full of small explosions as he discharges the sound on a hiss of air and at times actually resembles a small locomotive and struts round the stage, hissing, whistling, huffing and puffing . . .

EDDY: So, I was spawned in Tufnell Park, that's no more than a
    stone's throw from the Angel, a monkey's fart from
    Tottenham or a bolt of phlegm from Stamford Hill . . .

Greek: Théâtre de la Colline, 1990

'Donc, j'ai été pondu à Tufnell Park, c'est juste à une jet à pierre du Angel, à un chouia de Tottenham où une giclée de glaviots de Stamford Hill . . .'

The audience laughter also seemed to hit every note in the chromatic scale . . . laughter in wheezes, shocks, mock shocks, disbelieving giggles, all varieties of groans with laughter as if saying, 'Ah, non, you can't be telling us that' . . . For a moment I felt like an English Rimbaud setting off a series of shock waves in the audience, as if I were physically able to tickle all of them, embrace all of them at once, and they all giggle and squeal in my arms. I've not heard this laughter before and it feels good. They listen intently as Eddy recalls the liturgy of public enemies that have tried to forestall him: stupidity, ugliness, violence, repression, political chicanery, the mob, English food, the pub . . . Richard enunciates *'le pub'* as if he were expelling a slow belch. I turn and examine the packed French audience, youngish, alert, keen and watching with a fascinated attention. The wife and mother of Eddy handles the text with consummate and sinewy ease and the scene of the sphinx is a highlight of the play. I sat and watched it all unfold and could hardly believe that this play – which started life at the Croydon Warehouse via the Wyndham's Theatre, breaking its journey at the Half Moon and the Arts, shot down in flames by an hysterical critical response, with the honourable exception of Marina Warner in 1980, won all manner of awards in Los Angeles and then nearly caused apoplexy in the lily livers of New York reviewers, who fled screaming into the street, adapted for opera with the stunning music of Mark-Anthony Turnage – was now playing in a large theatre in Paris with critical acclaim and had won a 'Molière' award for Best Play.

In Paris the public vote for the play, not a few simpering 'experts', therefore it was all the more satisfying that France, home to Molière, Corneille, Rostand, Feydeau, Sartre, Genet, should now find a place for Berkoff. Ah, they have such taste, the French!

Fiji . . . 1990

One of those calls from LA. 'Do you want to play a Nazi in Fiji?' I thought, oh no! After Hitler you can go no further, and I was inclined to decline. However, it did coincide with a trip to LA to direct Acapulco *and I thought why not – it is merely a few thousand miles further west. I stayed eight weeks and it was relatively painless, although even to this day the film has never been exposed to the light of day – was it that bad!?*

Wake up with a piercing trill of bird song . . . the stars are still shot into the sky like diamonds and so the atmosphere must be clear. The morning's backdrop slowly lightens from a deep, dark navy, as the clouds take shape and the dawn filters through the darkness, seeping into the inky squid blue . . . tall thin palms cut a silhouette against the sky as they lean into the sea.

Fiji . . . a tropical island country set in the Pacific bursting with white explosive smiles as the natives flash their famous welcomes. I'm on an Ozy (Australian) picture about the young life of one of its famous heroes, Errol Flynn, who in his early pre-Hollywood days was an adventurer seeking gold in New Guinea, and Fiji is doubling for New Guinea, being a little less dangerous and unpredictable. This is one of those magic carpet jobs when an actor suddenly finds himself plucked out of a grey back-street in Hackney and flung into an exotic location, like the whirlwind in *The Wizard of Oz*. However, this time this actor is plucked from LA for a twelve-hour flight which really seemed just another hop around the Pacific. Qantas Airways ('we have never lost a plane') was preparing me for what was to come as I settled myself into my paid-for first-class seat. Two pleasant middle-aged duffers, who would have looked quite at home in a back-street bar in Sydney's King's Cross, were our stewards. Their jackets flapped over the food as they served it, trying to hold their coats with one hand and scoop up the trifle with the other or spilling champagne all over me and offering to give me a chit for the cleaning bill. It was the worst service in my life and I couldn't think it was any advantage over some pleasant females who take up less room in a restricted space, who move with more grace and wear fitted clothes that don't flap in your food and are quite frankly certainly better to look at during a ten-hour flight. I mean, there are horses for courses. Soon as I hit Fiji I am immersed in Australasia. This is on the way to becoming an Ozy Majorca and the place is teeming with pot-bellied chaps wearing shorts, knee-length white socks and polished shoes . . . it's most efficient in the heat without losing dignity and the effect is sobering after LA and their body obsession, daily gym work-outs in the pursuit of lithe everlasting bodies. Here in Fiji they let it all hang out and grab a fag, smoke as they get out of the water, but at least they are healthily earnest, pink-faced tourists and snorkelling unspoilt kids with high-pitched twangy voices that seem to be always going up the scale. However, it is a violent contrast from the new thinking in LA which is at most trying to embrace the new liberalism, guard against any sign of racist, sexist or other discriminatory stance and preach the values of new-age thinking in general from vegetarianism to non-smoking.

At least here the Ozy crew are not obsessed by the grosses and losses on movies and are content merely to try and make a good pic. The conversation by the edge of the pool is taken over by a couple of ockers who have been glued to their chairs all day knocking back the booze and talking the kind of colonial crap that I was spared in the USA but which is so prevalent among all walks of life in England and Oz. Especially by those who never live anywhere but in their own stew and therefore taste nothing else except the occasional forage to Majorca or Fiji where they not only take their culture with them but can indulge in its worst elements. So here, as we order our rum punches, the talk varies, but at the lower end it's very funny as the two ockers gab about booze, money and of course we couldn't get through an hour without thrashing the 'Abos' . . . then it was back to how much booze we sank the night before. 'I really thrashed the room service last night,' he boasts. 'I was drunk as a bat and I kept trying to get through and order a burger . . . in the end nine hamburgers came up, of course I ate them all!' They sat all day drinking and telling hilarious anecdotes and I wondered about their brains, their livers and all other bodily functions. When a good-looking young woman walked past they went into a fit of expletives, digging inside themselves for verbal protection to wall themselves up against the knowledge that she would never in a million years be theirs, unless of course she was raped. And so with much Ozy wit, which put me in mind of the Irish, they flogged the Chinese café owners in Sydney, Abos, women and all human elements that they would or could not co-mingle with while downing vast quantitites of booze, but I suspect that the almighty binge is a simple desire to try and find some element of a real human being that retreated a long time ago.

The crew are a friendly and easy-going bunch and work together like a team, united by the director, whom they all respect, so it's not going to be painful. I walk into the co-ordinator's office to collect my per diem; the co-ordinator looks up with a friendly smile. 'You had a shit yet?' I was slightly nonplussed by this solicitous and rather frank concern for my bodily functions, after my long flight, I supposed. While I admired her Ozy candidness, to be absolutely sure I questioned . . . 'Did you say, did I have a shit yet?' She apologized and repeated the question . . . 'Have you had a *schedule*?' . . . Ah, the accent can cause confusion at times.

Started work today in a mock New Guinea bar built over a river, a kind of sleaze-pit where the old gold prospectors would sit and rot and tell tall stories. There's a wide river nearby which I keep yearning to plunge into as I sit and sweat and wait for action. The Fijians seem eternally happy, especially the village people, and they sit and watch me with their children and are totally mesmerized and giggle at my antics.

The natives laugh infectiously and are natural story-tellers, and as one of them recounts an event the others start whooping and screaming with laughter. This seems to be their chief source of entertainment for each other. They look at you and greet you with your name – even if they have just heard it they never forget it. They earn very little from the hotels and share what they do get amongst the village. Food is taken from the plantations and fish is taken from the sea and so they have no need for shops except for salt or tea and their own brew called Kava, which is made from the Kava root pulled out of the earth, dried and beaten into a powder which is mixed according to strength with water and then drunk ceremoniously. Since it is not fermented and yet seems to send the men to sleep it must contain some kind of narcotic, although very mild.

In the compound somebody found a very small kitten and we all went to its rescue, although small creatures are being dropped all over the island. Our assistant director cut a plastic cup down to an inch and poured milk into it. The Fijians watched, much amused by our concern. The kitten wolfed it down with great relish and then was fed some cake, which it also ate hungrily, and later in the day I dropped some cake into some milk which it devoured, and then, young as it was, it ran under one of the huts and did its business since now it had something to do! It was a beautiful sight to see it behaving like a real cat seeking privacy for its ablutions and not a starved rag of skin and bone scratching around.

John Savage, the actor, joins us from some far-off country and brings his girlfriend who is playing a small part in the film as Flynn's native lover. She tells us she is writing songs about child-abuse, thus demonstrating her very worthy credentials. She has a topless scene with our hero and puts a dab of spit on her nipples to keep them perky for the shot, licking each palm with a quick dab to apply it. I'm playing a German villain who tries to seduce Errol Flynn into working for the Nazis, and the gratuitous homosexual overtones, given Flynn's predilection, make little sense. Sometimes a film makes no sense at all and suddenly I am tired of it and of hanging about, filling in time with scuba-diving, being lonely, seeking out drifting conversation.

The mornings are beautiful and I rise early to breakfast before the crew get there just to watch the deep blue turn liquid aquamarine and be shot through with red streaks as the clouds are set on fire by the rising sun. A giant reef surrounds most of the island and you can walk out for a mile and swim at high tide and have no fear of sharks since it's too shallow. I swam and walked and marvelled at all the divine creatures in the world as I explored the underwater world with my goggles, awed at the incredible brightness of colour of the fish, and on the way back a woman was gathering what seemed like stunned or dead fish out of the sea.

Apparently she strikes the water with a poisonous root and within a short time all the fish in that area drop dead, since the poison interferes with their breathing and they twitch a few times and then die. Suddenly all that sparkling, brilliant life had gone out of the creatures; all those flickering spurts of colour were now corpses and the beautiful inedible angel fish died for nothing, but most of the fish she put into a basket and will have fish stew for a long time. After a moment I decided to help her, since I spotted a few under some rocks and I had the goggles to see, and so she gave me a spike to pull them out from where they lay under some reefs and I crawled under. On crawling out I started to float up and caught my back, but was so excited to be getting the fish that I didn't pay any attention to my skin being scraped off. Sitting under a palm tree I feel its tough bark comforting me and hear the sweetest music in the whole world. Polynesian music sung by four big Fijians, each singing in a different key, creating the most dulcet chords, high-pitched and almost softly feminine; the sea rushes in and mixes its rasp with the voices and the wind is warm and embracing.

We are shooting into the nights now and the stars are bulging in wild profusion over the island. John Savage is only here for three days, to help ensure an American release, and I'm pleased to meet the man whose performances lit up the screen in *The Deerhunter*, *Salvador* and *Coming out of the Ice* . . . Savage is the representative for American angst, usually playing characters who are emotionally stripped bare to the wire and uncompromising; and, bizarrely, he has chosen to spend a lot of his life in South

Africa. It's Saturday night and the Fijians from the nearby village of Lassie Lassu sit in a group and contentedly watch and are suitably awed by our strange machines. The mother grips the little ones between her knees and the chickens scratch around happily and with such commotion that Frank Howson, the director, has to ask them to keep the clucking down. A native grinds some coconut in his teeth and throws some to the birds, who are thereafter content. After we finish shooting I notice the natives have a habit of imitating us to their great amusement. I see the importance of theatre for them and how in the villages it would keep alive their history and be a stabilizing influence and a guide to their past, since theatre was there before the printed word.

All the Ozies smoke at breakfast. They seem to think it quite natural to puff away after their bacon and eggs, and they play a lot of games in the pool, one of which is knocking your opponent off a log that straddles the water. You are equipped with a soft wet cushion and you whack it across your opponent's face until he falls in. I think if there were crocs in the pool it might be more interesting.

Last night we came to a bridge where a group of boys were wildly signalling to us, and so the make-up artist José and I got out, thinking they were wanting to show us a huge fish, but instead we saw that a car had crashed over the bridge and was now lying belly-up in five feet of water, its wheels strangely still and the occupant trapped within. A group of Fijians were already trying to push the car right side up. More cars were turning up and José had the bright thought of turning his car headlights on the river scene, and the native women were screaming and shouting with horror as if watching a spectacle that was not real but staged, and the headlights gave it all a strange theatrical look, and more Fijians had descended from the bridge and all were heaving and pushing to get the car over while the side-lighting from José's car rendered everything more dramatic. The water was chest-high and seething as the arms of the men threshed and heaved the car to go over, but it was stuck and the occupant no doubt expanding within the water. I debated with myself whether to make a gesture and lend some muscle and curiously felt self-conscious about what would be such a normal act of aid, but before I could act the car had turned over accompanied by a huge cry. The women screamed again as each movement progressed towards the uncasing of the occupant, who must be dead by now. Perhaps his life was hanging by a thread that would snap in seconds and my arm may have loaned the seconds necessary. Another huge cry went up as a jemmy prised the door, which swung open. Now the brown bodies were waiting since only one could get inside, and he pulled at the unseen body but could only pathetically come up with his sock and then brought up a shoe. The women screamed again. The thread of his life had certainly snapped by now and he would be floating in Davy Jones, but there is still hope, and hope fired the muscles, but he couldn't be pulled out since he must have not only been heavy but was in the driver's seat which was still in the river. Again the bodies formed a fresco in a Greek tragedy, pushing, heaving, shouting to each other in Fijian . . . 'push, push, push' . . . and the car rocked and rocked in its muddy grave, and again the car was turned, and now on its wheels to the accompanying screams of the women who became a chorus of bacchantes or furies. The driver's door was forced open and this time two of the men were bleeding severely from the attempt and broken glass. Now the moment had come to pull the dead or nearly dead man out of his tomb. This was the cue for the women to start screaming in earnest as if they were watching a Hollywood movie and a grave were being exhumed, and slowly like a soft creature being eased out of its shell the man was pulled out. His arms appeared and then a huge belly and six men carried him to a tree and rested for a while and tried pumping him, but then moved him to the bank where he might be taken to hospital.

He resembled a huge white fish on the river bank. The crowd moved around him like a swarm of bees and José said, 'Yes,' when I said, 'Can you give the kiss of life?' José, a Spaniard who has lived most of his life in Australia, goes to the prone body and a group of wet brown bodies pushing the man's legs back and forwards, and my mind begins a frenzied search for all the half-digested bits of information regarding what to do in such terrible circumstances – and what you do is usually wait for someone who does know what to do. They were still pumping the man's legs back and forth, who looked rather dead than alive, his eyes slightly open and somehow gunged up and his tongue held between clenched teeth. José bent down and I felt sick for him. The man's nose was a froth of the emissions from his lungs and throat and José had to plant his live mouth on his. He asked for something to wipe the man's face and somebody threw a shirt, and he wiped the man's face and then put his warm human lips to the man's cold, dead-looking mouth. He breathed into him again and again but nothing happened. He thumped his chest and we all waited but nothing happened. José seemed to know what he was doing, he used to work in a hospital . . . while I pathetically held the dead man's hand and tried to feel his pulse. I still kept thinking somehow that all was unreal and an extension of the movie we were just shooting. The man's hand was surprisingly soft and yielding, as if he needed to feel a friendly grip, and worst of all it was as warm as a live hand, he could have been merely sleeping. The crowd bent over José and waited for a reward for all their efforts in the water, but nothing happened. Eventually José gave up and said get him to a hospital and we departed, watching the huge brown body being transported by many of his countrymen. The bridge narrows suddenly from a wider road and he had overshot the bridge.

We went back to the hotel and drank rum punches and suddenly everybody seemed amazingly alive to me, as if we were all dead bodies in *reality* but animated by some miraculous energy that made us function. Life itself seemed like a shadowy substance, all so easily snuffed out, and I will never forget the dark waters and brown bodies thrashing in the foaming river as the desire to save a precious life was the most intense feeling anyone could have, and the centipede of arms and legs were as one being, and he was a limb of that being.

The film ended with a wrap party* and a rave-up and I actually got to dance, and everybody was happy that it had ended, and the director was pleased with the rushes, and I got to swim in that lovely river in the last shot of the film and was put on the plane for the ten-hour journey back to LA, altogether a memorable time.

*Literally when you wrap up a film.

The New York Times . . . 1990

I passed through New York after LA. Acapulco, *my play in the small Odyssey Theater, came and went.* Coriolanus *is just a memory but a memory still talked about and* Metamorphosis *has finished its limited run – I am here to talk to Ted Mann at the Circle in the Square Theater and spend the day wandering up Eighth Avenue. Each avenue is a history and culture on its own – you might be sailing up the Amazon and watching the extraordinary species that inhabits the river and its banks as you stroll up Eighth Avenue. The variety of its life never ceases to fascinate.*

A young man is digging inside a pay-phone with a long wire and fishing out nickels and quarters. He is thrusting his wire in and out with fevered desperation, barely protected by the small partition on each side where other phoners are ignoring him and getting on with their chat. Nobody is making any more than the slightest acknowledgement as the insane digger is raping the phone box with his piece of twisted wire. I stare at him, thinking as usual what to say, but in the meantime the small ferret of a man leaves and scuttles rat-like round the corner. Cross Eighth Avenue, or Avenue of the Americas as it's significantly called, and am jostled by weekend shoppers pouring in and out of the overstuffed delis. A basketball game is in progress whose frenzy always attracts a crowd of gaping spectators. The centre of attention is a black guy with an Afro haircut a yard wide who is bouncing around the court like a high-speed doll, his hair waving from side to side. All the participants are screaming directions to each other to pass the ball. These courts are just set off the pavement and are not only therapeutic for out-of-work men but provide much entertainment for passers-by. The cages are made of wire and resemble cages in a zoo. The players are nearly always black and muscled like panthers and always screaming at each other. Basketball courts seem to be a feature of American life, where old building lots are designated as squares for activities, and they help to release a great deal of murderous energy.

In front of the court a group of street vendors have taken advantage of the spectators and have spread their wares on the pavement, mostly old issues of *Life* magazine or other such faded gems, and I pick up a rare copy featuring the work of Laurence Olivier. There seem to be more and more of these poor 'marts' over the city, squalid little areas lined with old coats, books, second-hand debris of all kinds and the usual old mags like *Esquire* and *Life* that you could never normally afford, all flapping in the wind until a sudden rain reduces everything to a sodden mess.

There seems in recent years to be a plague of gigantism since vastly obese people populate the street; giant-arsed creatures wobbling down the avenue wearing yards and yards of denim, since this is the mandatory uniform for the ma and pa Ubus. Never have I seen such gargantuas of flesh containing such psychopathic needs to devour. Invocations to eat are thrust at you in every corner of the city, almost every step you take is an invitation to avail yourself of something to stuff in your mouth lest your journey be traumatized by sensory deprivation. I take a coffee and watch the world slither by. A family are taking a constitutional stroll since it's the Jewish holidays, and there are a lot of casual strollers wearing jackets and ties.

There is a mother and father of 'normal' size whose plain daughter has succumbed to 'Michelinism' and wobbles down the street swathed in her tyres of flesh and the uniform denim jeans. She is not as vast as some, but huge enough to begin to have trouble walking without the wobble. They stroll down the village, trying to be an ordinary family taking a constitutional, belying the pain and neurosis that must go on inside their four walls. When you stroll here you have to wear that air of sprightliness that all is OK and pretend not to notice every few yards some ex-human propped against a wall as he rots away caked in layers of filth and grime. You have to stroll and not look, but I cannot help but look, and stare with grim fascination. Over a decade ago these sights were more prevalent in the Bowery and lower East Side but now the army of the poor and homeless is creeping upwards into the entrails of the city and the little village parks resemble refugee camps.

The afternoon casts shadows over faces that stare out of the gloom. Black faces whose haunted eyes gaze out at the world passing by as if they were some alien race. Do not look and confirm them in their state, for if you do not maybe they do not exist and the desolate figures themselves will come to think that they are invisible.

In a small park two attractive-looking and healthy girls are having a picnic in the middle of the camp of the homeless and are quite happy, having found an unoccupied table, and easily ignore the shards of humanity in the background. I walk on and up the avenue and see a man and woman who are both reasonably dressed half fighting and half holding on to each other as if the world were in the middle of an earthquake. The man staggers away and the woman throws him against the wall and he seems powerless to resist, and they stare at each other intensely as drunks do, as if trying to balance on the tightrope between their staring eyes. They stagger a few more yards and the sequence is repeated.

I head on and examine the titles in a giant video outlet but holding up the wall of the shop is the decaying body of a vagrant who is scratching himself furiously as if he were being eaten alive, while opposite in the Chinese restaurant sit couples politely eating their lunch and a woman is wearing a hat like you did in restaurants in the fifties. They are directly opposite the scratcher. I cannot help but photograph the pain etched in his face, and I circle him as you might a dying beast whose mortality fascinates. He seems to be totally unaware of me.

An actor passes by who was once in a play of mine called *Kvetch* and who then repeated his performance in NY where the play was murdered by the critics. He looks dressed up and formal since he's just been to the 'gay' synagogue for Yom Kippur.

He was astonished, he tells me, at how conservative the service was, and I think about gays being devout in a synagogue while he thought the service would be more 'theatrical' . . . as we talk a giant 'Michelin' slides his huge carcass out of a car and finds a stool at the White Horse Tavern where young Dylan used to knock back the booze. I walk on past the screaming cars and screeching tyres, and howling radios blasting from the open windows of mobile cassette decks which you sit in rather than carry. The papers cover Friday's deaths, and even they are particularly appalled by the death of a car driver attacked by two other drivers for some minor quibble and left there on the road, where he was run down. As he crawls, mortally wounded, to a kerb, the whole street's horns are screaming for him to get a move on. I walk on away from the noise of the village and see a man across the road leaning against the wall in a helpless posture as if to say: What the hell am I doing here? Above him is the ironic sign 'HOME BANKS'. I photograph him from the opposite side of the road. He is leaning on his elbow and twisting from side to side. I cross the road and feel I ought to explore this mystery of why I am walking and why he is lying on a filthy pavement. I imagine the few coins I drop will allow me audience with the representative of the aliens for a few moments. 'Where are you from?' 'The Bronx, you know near the concourse.' 'How did you get here, like this?' He replies in a weary but determined way, 'I'm not a drunk, everybody thinks I'm a drunk and wants to put me away but I have a nervous disease which affects my balance . . . everybody thinks you're drunk just because you're on the street . . . no, I'm not drunk.' He sounds articulate and has a firm voice and seems repairable, if this wasn't a throwaway society. He seems a man with some humour left, and irony. His name is Kirwin. I leave him against his wall and walk on, mounting the gradual rise on Fifth Avenue. Opposite the huge stores the poor are more organized. 'I AM WITHOUT FOOD AND HOMELESS AND NEED HELP.' This man sits on a stool in front of a table as if he were collecting on behalf of the general poor. A large jar sits on the table. He sits and frames a crooked smile as I pass. I keep passing them: the standing or sitting beggars, or people just standing by some corner and not even begging, just standing in a drift, unable to move as if their battery had worn down. The constant mantra follows your footsteps . . . 'Got any change . . . Could you spare a little change, sir . . . I haven't eaten for three days . . . Have you

the price of a coffee . . . Sir, have you some food money . . .
Could you . . . would you . . . please, sir, have you . . . I need
. . . help me . . .'

The warm shadows of the autumn nights cover it all in a soft
veil and soften the sin of poverty. My taxi ride bumps over the
broken spine of Eighth Avenue.

A homeless bum steps up to the window as we stop at the red.
'Got a little change, sir, for some food, please, I haven't eaten for
two days . . .' The taxi driver stares ahead and mentally eggs on
the green and hits the gas. 'Those bums are lazy bastards . . .
don't wanna work . . . only wanna drink.' We approach the
Forties and Fifties; hell is warming up and its guardians are
keeping watch outside the bus station looking as if they are
waiting for Godot. I once said that ports to a country are like
entrances to the body, but no less are bus stations to the city
meeting places for all the germs that enter and exit the body of a
city. A black man is moving as if in slow motion and using the
shop windows as if to guide him to some inexorable destination
outside Hades. He seems more than drunk and more than stoned
or maybe just high on crack. Further up the avenue we come to
theatre-land and pass 'Live Male Shows' and groups of transients
slumped around Times Square and gassing. It must be a meeting
place for sinister transactions. I descend into the maelstrom of
Saturday night in New York and everybody is on the boil,
heading in all directions for their pleasures. It's determined
energy that seethes all over the sidewalk. I head to the Circle in
the Square Theater run by formidable Ted Mann who has run a
tight ship for thirty years and where I once saw George C. Scott
give an enthralling performance in *Death of a Salesman* and no less
a one in Noël Coward's *Present Laughter*. Opposite the modern,
cool-looking theatre where the crowds are already gathering is a
doss-house for transients called Mansfield House, and the usual
gathering of unemployed vagrants and drunks plus small-time
dealers make a flurry in the lobby. I cross the road and see the

faces of the great actors on the wall – they have paid a high price for their fame by the eight shows a week in which they are obliged to turn on their brilliance. The theatre is in the round, and on entering I feel sanity returning to my blood and brain, as if I had been starving. The theatre is full and everybody is in a state of expectation. It is so quiet when the actors enter and the lines of Molière in crisp translation ring out. It is Molière's devastating satire on the pathology of greed, *The Miser*. It is superbly played by the company and led by the formidable Philip Rosco. Meanwhile, outside . . .

Sunday with Joe Papp . . . 1989

Unlike some producers I have worked for, and that is most, Joe cared for his directors and actors and one day invited me to his house in the Connecticut countryside. Joe Papp was one of the world's great entrepreneurs – he inspired many actors, directors and writers and placed his very humane values over everything he did. His death in 1990 saddened me greatly. I was in New York directing Coriolanus.

Wet Monday, the city is cracking up; the roads bulge and sag, spilling themselves over the kerb like slabs of chocolate over a cake or like molten lava. In the road great moon-like craters appear where the tar has been sucked down by the steam that belches out from the cracked pipes. Makeshift iron plates cover the holes as if the city were plastering over its chancred face. Never have I seen such floods after a mild rainfall: the drains are blocked with garbage and you leap and dodge around mini-lakes. A taxi ride roller-coasters over potholes and you suffer a teeth-rattling faulty suspension. The city seems to be in a permanent state of decay and its decline seems irreversible. It is diseased beyond redemption, both physically and spiritually, so it was with some relief that the idea of a country trip suggested by Joe was taken up.

I think eating together draws you together as friends, and the idea of a day in the country was often broached but never taken up. It seemed a long way to go, and if the chat gets difficult you are stuck. However, I hit Grand Central Station, which is the most marvellous ornament of high-domed Gothic splendour and a sheer marvel of architecture. Your eyes lift to heaven to behold the wonders of the great industrial age when trains were like stately queens and the stations grand palaces, but then they lower themselves and you see the poor and the desolate, the homeless and lonely huddled together on benches that were intended for the worthy travellers. The shock is incredible.

After arriving at the entrance, no courtyard, no area to disembark; just arrive off the street and be greeted by a bevy of shoe-shine boys who block your view of the famous plaque which celebrates the history and creation of the station. A few down-and-out blacks impersonate station porters and hail a passing cab for the departing travellers. These 'porters' sally out, arms akimbo, while the taxi spots the customer anyway and pulls over.

The game is then for the 'porter' to get between client and cab and appear to be the link. The client, since the door is held open for him, is abashed into donating a dollar bill. It is a little scam that every down-and-out does in New York whenever people are leaving public places and are standing awaiting a cab. The other, more familiar one takes place at the traffic lights in the Bowery when on the red two guys leap out and start cleaning your window in the few seconds that exist before the green, in the hope you'll throw out some change. Yes, there are many ways to earn a buck in the land of free enterprise. I buy a coffee 'to go' in a cup with 'I (a red ♡) NY'.

Everybody here seems to be sucking on something, as if the short journeys one takes are unendurable without the nibble of oral reassurance in the shape of a bagel or coffee, or a slice of pizza, or a 'hero', a hot dog, or pretzel, and you get into the act and walk down the street clutching your little nibble of gratification.

I buy a ticket, and this is a bit of a thrill for me since it is the first time I have travelled by train in the USA. So, leaving the hundreds bedded down for the day in the warm sanctuary of the station, I board my train and am surprised to find that the seats all face one way like sitting on a plane: the carriage stinks of urine since the toilet is quite close and probably doesn't function too well. The train slides mercifully out of the station and the city changes from fated slum to idyllic country hamlet with familiar white washboard façades on the New England-style houses.

The rain was pouring down when I alighted, but Gail, Joe Papp's wife, was waiting to pick me up at the station and we drove to their country retreat, which turned out to be a simple but comfortable wooden log cabin with lots of ground and distant, misty wet views of the surrounding country. They have the kind of view that other famous weekend dwellers, like Philip Roth, Baryshnikov and Pacino, probably look out on.

Joe welcomes me and offers me a beer. We crack some nuts,

although I wouldn't mind some grub or a hot coffee, but I make do with the cold beer, and we talk about guns and the notorious gun lobby (the National Rifle Association). Around here you are allowed to shoot deer with a bow and arrow, but no gun! I suppose such quaint refinements in the killing sport protect the residents from a mob of gun-crazy zombies roaming the countryside with a vital gene missing in their brains that enables them not to see anything sick in the killing of a few defenceless deer. A few days earlier I had seen, for the second time, a young deer strapped to the roof of a car, its tongue lolling down the window. I ran to the window and shouted, 'Arsehole!' They looked out, sullen and murderous. Joe says he keeps a rifle on the premises to feel safe. In the USA I can understand this need. This is a place to arm yourself.

Then we headed out to catch a matinée of a friend of Joe's, a musical, in a local town at a kind of art centre where smoking is forbidden in the lobby and only coffee served at the intervals. It was sloppily staged but well-sung, about the low life, based on a book by the same author who wrote *Man with a Golden Arm*. The immensely easily pleased American audience lapped up the simple tale, an insipid *Guys and Dolls*-type story. I have noticed how indiscriminating audiences here are, how they will guffaw at anything. I expect the mulch they are fed on the idiot box makes them feel that anything that is live and in the theatre is somehow cultured and worthy.

I remember some awful garbage called *Nuts* that was the first show I saw in LA and being astounded at the simple-minded 'yuk yuk' at the antics of the actors. Predictably it was made into a movie. The whole exercise this afternoon seemed to be a plea for a commercial exploitation, thus Joe's invite, and I, the unfortunate baggage he brought along. I was beginning to think of all the lovely things I could be doing in New York on a Sunday. Anyway, the crappy show allowed me to nod off and I sank into a blissful mini-sleep and when the first hour had been evacuated from my existence I promised myself a coffee. Fortunately and characteristically, Joe met our host in the interval with a candour that both surprised and educated me. 'It's terrible,' he said flatly and without rancour, 'and we can't stay, I have a meeting with a friend, and I can't sit through this, it's bad for my head . . .' All this said with firmness and humour so his young eager entrepreneur wouldn't be hurt. Our host was, in fact, the associate director of the Country Club Theater and so he wasn't miffed.

So we drove into the rain after catching a quick, picturesque glimpse of the Hudson . . . 'You can see Long Island from here . . .' and we joined the lasso of cars that wound their way along the grey misty freeway at about ten miles per hour. I was keeping venom at bay, but so far this was not my idea of my free day off.

We soon exhausted those trite areas of communication that strangers or slight friends have, where you scan the superficialities of each other's existence without quite getting down to the depths, as if you can't quite open those doors. So we talked shop, threw *Coriolanus* around, which had just opened to good reviews, talked old theatre, etc. . . . bore. When chat became exhausting, especially for Joe, since I had by now clamped up like a muscle spasm, Joe sang the remnants of half the songs in existence and Gail drove into the mysterious heartlands the wrong way until we landed in Connecticut. Discovering this, we found the way back miraculously, and all I could think of was catching the 9.30 p.m. train to New York, which now gave us only three hours more of each other.

I hadn't eaten since breakfast at 8 a.m. We soon got back and then Gail poured me a large Margarita and started to prepare dinner, which seemed to take an eternity, or maybe I was just starving by this time. I went on the porch to puff on a roll-up and watched the mists coming in and returned inside to wait for dinner. Joe somehow felt he had to entertain me and also let me know him better and started to tell me about the origins of the

Public Theater and how he discovered *Hair*. He was teaching at Yale one year and starting up the Public Theater which was then just a large room. A guy he chatted to on the train to Yale, on hearing this, offered some hand-written pages which were the basis for a musical he had written. It was about Vietnam and was an anti-war statement.

Joe was trying to decide what play should follow their first production, but when he heard the music he opened with *Hair* in a small off-Broadway theatre in 1968. The same year, and on the other side of the world in the Arts Laboratory, Drury Lane, I was to open my first production of Kafka's *In the Penal Colony* . . . so Joe and I started at the same time, but weren't to meet up until twenty years had passed. Joe relished his tale and told me that the guy kept writing more pages until the book was finished, and Galt McDermot wrote the music. One day Galt played something for Joe on the piano and it was the fabulous and uplifting 'This is the dawning of the age of Aquarius'. A convinced Joe then decided that this *had* to be the first show, and not *Armstrong's Last Goodnight*, a worthy play no doubt, but not likely to set theatres on fire around the world! *Hair* made the Public Theater *twenty-five million dollars*! More interestingly, Joe added that the famous nude scene that was such a feature of Tom O'Horgan's production, and which dominated the publicity in London, was never performed in the original production. Also the father, who was ridiculed and made to look an obsolete figure of fun and bourgeois uptightness, was in the original a simple and ordinary man in conflict with the new-found values of his son. The brilliant Shakespeare to music, 'What a piece of work is man', was added later, when McDermot had seen Joe's production of *Hamlet*, which followed *Hair*.

So Joe, like a Penelope, unravelled his early history, and it was fascinating and I was enraptured. By this time Gail had served up the dinner, the delicious remains of a Thanksgiving turkey. 'All organic,' she says, and it tastes it. I can actually savour ancient flavours. It's time to go, and again Gail drives me in her old car, which seems to perform to a bit of gentle vocal persuading. I catch the train and sit down-wind from the loo and with my stomach bursting with turkey. I was, in the end, very glad to have had Sunday in the country with Joe.

Salome . . . The Last Show . . . 1990

Salome *was my first major production at the National and was successful enough to transfer to the Phoenix Theatre. I loved the opulent splendour of the play, and the mystery. The last night came and there were riots up Charing Cross Road caused by Thatcher's insane, inept change in the rates laws. I could not help but reflect on the contrast between our delicate unfolding of* Salome *in slow motion and the mindless violence existing outside.*

Saturday was the last performance of *Salome* and I was looking forward to it. It was only a ten-week season but the going is hard when you go for it seven times a week, and expectancy was high. It was one of those actor's fantasies, to play Herod in one of the most exquisite plays of the nineteenth century, a play of word pictures that swim in front of your eyes like the paintings of Gustave Moreau, particularly his Salome cradling the head of the Baptist. Fantasy is reality made into your own image and brings with it longings and desires not so palpable in the real, ugly world. Reality is a kind of quotidian stodginess and a perception of the world photographically and materially, whereas fantasy or imagery connects the world to your own system of values. At the end of the nineteenth century there was an enormous rejection of the Victorian horrors of industry and a Wildean call for art for art's sake, and yet no matter how extraordinary Wilde's prose could be (particularly in his surreal fairy tales) there was an enlarged heart beating for the human spirit and for its imagery and dreams through words, particularly those written for the stage, and yet *Salome* was criticized for its specious content, its bejewelled shallowness, since the watchers weren't able to allow the images to form in their minds and the starved Brits are too sensually deprived to respond. It's as if the synapses and brain cells, starved for so long, can only connect real concepts and have no prehensibility to change the words into interior paintings. Hence our approval of static, deadly interpretations of Shakespeare and of wooden productions of the same. It's words that count, and yet words have the ability to produce all kinds of effects, and children are the fastest at making pictures in their minds and being moved, and as we age the picture gets drier and smokier until all that is left is the bare bones of meaning and we have the shape and skeleton but no hues of the flesh. The theatre, which is meant to be a visual art as well as spoken, has the

151

proscenium arch built high to allow giant pictures and epic events to unroll via the words, but now, and how apt, many theatres have lowered that arch, the picture frame, so that the pathetically small action taking place beneath on a sofa won't be too chilling in the vast cavern. Occasionally gestures are made, as if we realized that we are not blind yet and the senses and eyes also must be fed, as well as the ears with the onomatopoeia of words, and so sometimes a little dribble of spectacle is allowed to encroach and a 'movement' adviser brought in to stage a 'battle' scene, but these are encrustations and are not central to the whole, they are little flurries of lip service to the possibility of some kind of art. Usually we are perversely concerned about such ideas as theatre as an art, and regard that as rather a decadent approach left to weird outsiders that might stop us getting on with our amateur cricket. In such cases we might be more inclined to rubbish someone's work that smacks of something rather creative, to humiliate and assault it. If we can't do it, then let's show how awful we can be, and have a rare old laugh, fall on your arse, play it with hobnail boots, and don't take it too seriously for God's sake. The director sits on his bum and discusses the play and its exquisite entrails of meanings, enrapturing us with curlicues of wisdom, and we are bored, since this is only one part of the feast. The food may look good but it is tasteless. We evade the need for art by talking about 'writer's theatre', as if there were no 'theatre's theatre' in which writers are just the chefs. Producers scour the world for the next play which will bring some light into the dark, soggy world of under-used seats and shrill cries for more money, but there is a world out there which belongs to theatre and it is not about plays that could just as easily be seen on TV, which is equally in love with the sordid mirror-image of the time and the pedestrian Brownie camera version of life.

I am not sure that we have a fondness for line, form or movement, rather that we are in fact hostile to what cannot be read on the page and heard. We believe in the authenticity of realism in the true Victorian sense, and we are so sure that it is money that will save theatres, and not artists of vision, that there is a huge clamour for more of it, since money buys things like sets and pays for junk as well as wages. With more money, will we have better art, or just more . . . something or other? Who cares? We do not encourage visualists or artists in any medium, least of all the incinerators of TV, who obey the same old hierarchy of find the play, cast the actors, get your director and do it. One eminent TV producer asked to at least view *Salome* replied that unfortunately he had only one night off and was going to a Bowie concert. Thus he was at least honest as to his limitations and cultural philistinism. And yet this man was supposed to be scouring the world for material for the relentless tubes. We have left the Phoenix and returned it to Charing Cross Road, and the spirit of Wilde fuelled us for seventy glorious performances, and a piece of history was reborn almost a hundred years after it was written, and how vividly the lines resound today. The English love wit above all things and hence prefer Wilde's satiric comedies, but wit comes from a different part of the spirit and is inclined to debunk and dethrone, which is a vital function of language, albeit not too distant from its cousin, contempt.

On Saturday, while Wilde's web of conceit was being spun out for the matinée audience, it was continually shattered by the wow-wow-wowing of police sirens and black Marias shuddering to a screeching halt as a small army of malcontents were smashing and looting. The contrast was severe, between mindless violence, which is a form of impotence, and the battle of words on stage.

It was a sickening sight watching these pathetic creatures who had no means of expression except destruction. Destruction is easy but creation is hard.

New York Café on Third Avenue: Day 1 . . . 1989

There was a small diner on Third Avenue I went to a couple of times a week, just to vary my breakfast haunts. This one was a piece of New York history and I wanted to record it for posterity – I suppose I wanted to paint every detail of it as if I knew I would not be there much longer. When I walked down the avenue in February 1992 it had vanished for ever. Not even a small plaque celebrated its years of scrambled eggs and coffee. Gone, like it never existed!

Each morning I would choose a different café, and some I would cling to for a few days and then investigate another. There were so many of them, each with a distinct personality, each with its loyal group of arses propped on the mushroom bar-stools nursing a thick American coffee cup. There is no question that the American diner is a sanctuary of human warmth and comfort to a Brit starved of such easy accessibility to escape from the maelstrom of city life. Stopped today at one of my favourite cafés with a long tunnel-like interior and a food counter running the length of it. There were no booths, so you sat on the stools and made friends with the counter-hand. A fan whirled above me and behind there stood a grocery counter topped by a few ancient shelves. A real 'Norman Rockwell' café, with its impossible medley of features crammed into the confined space: shelves, grills, hot-plates, metal drawers, cake dishes with iced cakes on display under old and scratched plastic domes, a Kenmore microwave whose surface was a stage for cardboard cartons and packets of cornflakes with a game printed on the back of the packet called 'Find the President' . . . the back wall was dressed in a fancy chrome quilted effect to give a sharp, clean look which had prompted some artistic eye to paint the wooden shelf above it silver to blend in . . . a steel pipe runs along the back wall at the top to disappear in the corner into what looks like a gas container pinned to the wall . . . it must be gas, since another pipe snakes out to the central feature of the diner, which is a hot-plate upon which a mash of onions is being fried by the chef. I watch his back telling me about his concentration in the act, which he then finishes, and slopes off to the back room on my left at the end of the store. He is no doubt preparing the lunches in some strange private area, since the door is open but reveals only some shelves with a bizarre assortment of bric-à-brac that gathers dust for endless years . . . and a place to hang your jacket since a youngish man has just gone in, hung his coat, and emerges, closing the door to the secret junk room behind him.

The little cupboard-like rooms remind me of those places where workers sit eking out their 4 p.m. tea-break and smoke, and there is always a packet of biscuits around. Just then the old man cooked up some more onions on the hot-plate and re-entered the secret room, this time with several eggs, so the clues are getting hotter . . . the old man looks as if he might be dying and yet at the same time possesses an indefatigable spirit which sneaks out in his voice, which sounds like rusty metal. He wears one of those woollen cloth check shirts that are used by Ad-men to suggest dependability. He has now come round my side and sat himself at the counter to have a break. He just made me my breakfast, a soul-satisfying sandwich which ignited little memory cells of childhood.

Since he had run out of hash browns – 'big run on them this morning' – I asked for my childhood fantasy, which I watched him prepare with loving care . . . toasted cheese, tomato, lettuce and some sliced pickle glued together with mayo . . . he made it and then put it back on the hot-plate covered by a small weight like an old-fashioned iron to seal it. Then I ate it and it did taste of childhood and it was good. So good in fact that even in the eating I wanted to record it so as not to lose it and I found myself reaching for my pen like you reach for a camera to capture a vivid sunset or a painter reaches for his brush . . . so I, moved by the sandwich, wished to preserve the experience, and not let it fade in time, since you know that it must fade as surely as the old man in the plaid shirt is fading, and yet he now seems to be caught in this moment of time as if he might be here for ever. In that particularly American way everyone sits at the counter, since it is friendlier and you become for a while a part of that group, and if not, at least party to the back-and-forth bantering and gossip while the counter-hands hold the stage. A customer wearing a tweed hat with a black-edged feather stuck in the band sits reading his paper while munching on a turkey sandwich. Of course it is cold today, with a 'wind-chill factor up to twenty degrees below', so everybody has been asking for hash browns, those sliced potatoes that are singed brown on the hot-plate.

The old man sits down again at the end of the counter and takes out a cigarette, but he is only resting to write out the cards which he inscribes with the day's dishes and then pins them to the wall. The cards require some creative decisions and so the old man concentrates as he writes with a wide blue-and-red felt-tipped pen. After each item he underlines it with a small wave, since straight lines look clumsy done by hand, and so he makes a series of waves or little hills and the wave's crest is determined by the item that it underlines. Thus you have 'side orders' (a wavy hill), 'french fries' (a distant group of hills), 'potato salad' (hills), 'coleslaw' (wavy hills), 'macaroni salad' (wavy hills), 'mashed potatoes and gravy' (a rough sea with large crests), so this last one must signify the end of the small orders and gives an added frisson to the mashed potatoes, or it may have been by way of a drum roll to announce the next act, since written underneath was 'home-made spinach pies' (small distant hills) and then the last, 'home-made soup de jour', end of card. The old man, having accomplished his task, now avails himself of a chicken sandwich I saw him make earlier, which he cuts in four pieces accompanied by a bowl of baked beans. He sits two seats to my left and the ketchup bottle is on my right. He gets up, crosses behind me and takes the bottle, returning to his seat, when it would have been nothing to ask me to pass it, but he didn't wish to disturb a customer. It's now 11.30 a.m. and a woman next to me taking an early lunch complains, rather too gently in my opinion, that the chicken casserole usually has vegetables. The counter-hand smiles sheepishly . . . 'Yeah, he usually puts in peas and carrots' . . . without explaining the strange omission of these ingredients today and thus leaving the customer and myself deeply frustrated. 'Still,' he adds after a moment of intense deliberation to

mature the following thought, 'rice is a vegetable.' The disappointed woman answers with a much shorter pause, hence
testifying to her faster and unclogged brain-cells, 'No, it's a
starch,' but continues eating the stodgy goo of rice, chicken and a
creamy, starchy-looking sauce. Near the hot-plate is the coffee
machine with three coffee pots of water. Starting to crowd up
now, and so I pay and leave. The old man shouts down to the
cashier what I should pay and I escape into the swirling cold wind
of Third Avenue.

New York Café on Third Avenue: Day 2 . . . 1989

The discussion on the merits of hash browns versus french fries. Sometimes in New York diners I would feel like a visitor from space, observing at close quarters the inhabitants of a strange world.

Back in the little café, the snow has been flickering down and the windows are steaming up. The old man talks like one of those characters from a forties movie; he's lively this morning, with that wry cynicism he wears as one who has seen them come and go. I want to talk to him but he seems too real and I am too remote, as if I am watching a movie. At my stool I am the audience and watch the act but now he's retreated to the back room where I hear him coughing his guts up. He smokes too much behind the counter and has a real drinker's snout, a ripe, veiny, carbuncle. The morning is very *New Yorker* magazine of the forties, full of snow, yellow cabs, snow boots and people sitting in diners reading the papers and talking about the game last night. The counter is full and the colours are browns and greys. The radio is pouring out the saccharine music and the chewing-gum voices of the commercials. It sits atop one of the three giant fridges behind me, which are stuffed with fruit juices, beer and various sodas.

This morning saw a large, well-fed fluffy cat with a confident tail that shot up in the air like a geyser and curled over its sleek back. It had such a perfect erect spire of fur, large amber eyes, and it mooched around, opened the toilet door with its paw and, having checked it out, made a series of leaps, first on to the food counter near the door behind me. (The old man has just emerged from the secret room with a tray of bacon that seems more like slices of fat, with the merest suggestion of meat-like flecks standing out like coral islands in a sea of lard.) Then the cat leapt upwards towards its eyrie, poised – on the cold storage next to the chocolate-chip cookies – and eyed for a moment the uppermost plateau where sits the radio. Its large clear amber eyes scanned this distance to the top of the fridge whose contents revealed among other delights 'sun-sweet prune juice', which I made a mental note to buy. '*It's slippery but it's not bad,*' a large voice boomed out of the large unshaven face of a man whose authoritative tones suggested he dealt with his problems and had little use for 'sun-sweet prune juice' . . . so the cat wiggles its arse for take-off, which action betrays the tiniest dash of anxiety, since its task, though familiar, with increasing age is not to be taken for granted . . . so the wriggling goes on, the nose pointed upwards, the calculations computed and . . . leap! It made a good landing on its soft pads and proceeded to position itself in the hot regions where the air is a soup of coffee, bacon fat and hash browns. It sits in front of the speakers and surveys its kingdom. It reminds me of a jaguar poised on a rock in some primitive African landscape.

Eventually the old man tells me that he has worked here over thirty years, but actually twenty years in this place and ten years when the café was across the street. I'm surprised, since this café looks tired and older than its twenty years, but suppose they shifted some old fittings. Then there is a handsome, well-built and weight-trained assistant who has just come in, and I think it's a dead-end for someone so personable, but perhaps he's happy just to have some work. He's wearing a Hawaiian-style shirt with short sleeves. The radio is telling us: *'Sixteen-year-old crack smoker kills his mother in the Bronx for some alleged restriction.'*

There are sixteen stools at the counter and they're nearly all topped with an arse. The radio says it's twenty-two degrees Fahrenheit. The white tray of bacon has now been pulled out of the grill and is swimming in fat, which the old man takes and pours into a metal jug for future gravies and flavouring, and so his day rolls on, demarcated into such sections. It's cosy here and the shop is beginning to empty, the old man keeps a cigarette burning most of the time in the ashtray, which sits at the end beneath the gas fitting and next to the scotch tape. Two calendars are hanging up, both with D & M Ice-cream Corp. The phone bursts into life for the first time. The old man goes to it and says, 'Arnold' . . . so, that's his handle . . . a male customer in a royal blue jacket sits down and asks for french fries but Arnold, not having any right now, discusses the french fries rather than seem

to be wanting . . . 'Do you know how many people ask for french
fries in the morning?' The customer, not being a psychic, fails to
answer Arnold's rhetorical question and so Arnold continues.
'Two or three people.' He answers his own question, and by now
the customer and I are on tenter-hooks to see where this line of
argument is taking us. 'That means' – Arnold goes on steadily to
his dénouement – 'You've got to keep the oil burning all morning
for just two or three customers . . . you burn the shit out of it.'
The customer and I have no answer to this technical expertise but
we are both satisfied with a response that was not without a spot
of drama. The man settled for hash browns.

Coriolanus and the USA . . . 1988

I was given to much soul-searching and social commentary in the USA. Being an alien gives you a continual bird's-eye view since you are not immersed within the bosom of the action or institutionalized to their ways. Your own background provides the template by which all else is measured. It's like having a built-in crap detector so one can never be swept into the hysteria of need that seems to pervade so many.

The USA is a fascinating and enormously greedy nation, whose attention span is of a child-like duration and whose values centre on seeing how much they can grab out of life, and they do this with an awesome energy. Even when ordering their breakfast you can hear their whiney needs as the liturgy of kiddies' tastes emerges. 'You've run out of onion bagels?' . . . the voice raised a few notes as it ascends the scale to where panic reigns.

When you cater to every need, there is a danger of turning a virile race of people into a bunch of spineless drips. To tap the mystical dollar, entrepreneurs inject into the American body so many tastes, such a variety designed to appease every solitary bud on the tongue, that whoever absorbs this also develops a thousand different needs, the absence of even one of which will cause temporary breakdown. The breakfast arrives and I watch the recipient of these goodies express no gleam of thanks. No earthy hunger, just a sullen acceptance. One cries, 'Eggs over easy' (what a soft, infantile expression), and when I take my laundry in . . . 'How do you want it? Fluff and fold?' All swishy nursery yap. The spine wilts until, at last, what was the great tradition in America of a pioneering and gritty determination, plus entrepreneurial skills, is left to the Koreans, whose stoic-faced dignity seldom leaves them as they sit for hours guarding their treasury of sliced fruit and vast displays of salads that you buy by weight and take out. They sit for hours as the light burns through the night . . . all night . . . twenty-four hours. Just in case you need to get up in the middle of the night for a raisin muffin or pint of milk to still the crying of a raging ulcer.

TV caters to every whim, panders to every desire, markets the needs of loneliness by telling you to dial a number advertised on your twenty-four-hour channels, where every vicissitude of human experience is spoon-fed into you. Products come in packages or promises of fulfilment in the shape of a beautiful woman whom you are conned into believing is waiting for you for the price of a phone call at three dollars for the first minute. For your higher consciousness, you have the begging TV channel: PBS (Public Broadcasting System). They are liable to show worthy programmes which are, in the main, commercial-free, which is a relief, since the constant and increasing battering of 'messages' drives one completely insane and the commercials themselves are delivered very often in screaming, wide-mouthed shrieks, as moms have orgasms over the contents of a fruit pie. You are beaten over the head, since the ears are already worn out and the eyes deadened to the endless invocations to buy, so like those deafened by repetition, the shouts are louder.

The non-commercial TV is a relief, even if you are given a constant parade of animals in wild nature settings, accompanied by lush string music, as if the animals were a kind of nature's Twyla Tharp Dance Company. After the programme we are so 'awed' by the lack of commercials that for a full five minutes an earnest woman begs for contributions to keep the only 'culture' programme alive. It seems one has to beg for what is after all civilized and decent and remote from the filth of violence or shredded by the pollution of commercials. So I see what rampant capitalism is; it is a total disregard for human values or civilization. It seeks market values for everything. Small wonder that with such non-critical market-seeking pulp such venomous trash should crawl out of the dung heap as the like of TV evangelists. The Jim Bakers and his Medusa-like hag. So coarsened, so pulped are the brains of the mass audience, so reinforced with the simple images of sentiment, coupled with greedy need, that when another spokesman, selling his wares, preaches love and good, to draw in the bucks, there is no critical reaction to dismiss his claims or penetrate the stink of the nauseous couple. What would be laughed off the screen in the UK gets serious attention in the USA. Eventually the thieving frauds get found out, but what if they were not?

Coriolanus and the USA: 1988

This is the 'me first' land, not 'after you' . . . and 'arsehole' the appellative to fit all who deviate from your view. The 'me' drains all that is worthy in man and turns adults into retarded children and that is the most repulsive sight. The agonies of the child adult who has not learned to deal with and absorb his pain into adulthood is megaphoned in every bar and café in New York. Faces eagerly trade ears with each other, offering up their orifices like dustbins for the refuse of their lives if there are no willing shrinks who are only too glad to listen to you 'hurt' . . . I actually found this openness charming at first, as the caterwaul of the women in the Bagel Bake reiterated their scroll of agonies. Now I find it vaguely repellent, since it suggests a lack of fibre and stamina to deal with life and the threat is therefore implied that they would just as easily trample on you. The open wound. Self-satisfaction. Grossness. Lack of restraint.

An actor, in the company that I have so painfully and pains-takingly rehearsed, gives in his notice since he had another offer, and our run is only for seven weeks! Not seven months! His role is a major one and is central to the success of the play, and yet he is so blissfully unaware of any sense of moral integrity, so much a part of the 'me' society, that he will cause the entire overworked company to rehearse all over again to accommodate a new actor. Even Equity allows this abomination, since you are allowed to give two weeks' notice if you can grab more dough elsewhere. This means that actors will take a job and keep an eye out for another on the way.

So the texture of the play is ruptured by a self-seeking actor whose sense of ethics are as minute as his talent, and yet who can really blame him since this is a society where you trample on your fellow man? His wages were the normal off-Broadway scale. Joe Papp shrugs and dislikes it, but it has happened each time. The first, a helpless and useless performer, was given so much help from the leading actor that the lead almost had a nervous breakdown re-running the scenes until the new man felt confident. This uncertain actor was nursed and praised and in the end confessed that he had never had such help and love and blessed us all etc. So after we had all spilt blood to help him through, the mug gave his statutory two weeks' notice, and this after the reviews were closing us and there was only a further two weeks to go, so the understudy went on. I just couldn't believe he could have done it, but he did.

However, apart from the work, New York is still a feast and I can indulge myself, in my fantasy, in the amazing variety the greedy city demands for itself. A few nights after the actor gave notice, another actor – and a very good one – demanded the night off to attend his grandmother's funeral, and he careth not that the show was maimed badly since the understudy, who was playing a cameo, had to rush on, and so two vital roles were lost that night, while the actor had to attend his granny's funeral. No doubt she was very close and he missed her deeply, but he didn't care that the whole cast, plus audience, had to suffer for the granny's funeral and so in some way we were made to pay for his *feelings*. He is allowed to go because he threatens he will go anyway and because *feelings* are so important here, but it is *feelings* for *oneself*. I actually wonder if the production of *Coriolanus* that was so lauded in the press will even reach its modest run of seven weeks at this rate.

I began to admire the restraint of the Brits . . . their simple lives . . . a thin cheese roll in the break . . . an obsessive desire to be good in the theatre. An actor will go on if his house is burning down. The Brits take selflessness to the other extreme, but it is a safer place to be. In twenty years of directing I have never known an actor to leave before the end of a short run, except for one RSC small-part actor who was on loan to my group for a tour of Holland and was called back to do a tiny role and thus disrupted our show, where he had a great showy leading role. We reshuffled the parts and after an exhausting night we got through it. I suspected that the actor knew before he started on our tour that he could not make the last performance, but didn't want to miss a nice juicy tour. He was pissed every night anyway and this was for him a kind of watershed and a means of getting away from his wife. Unfortunately, so many English actors get blotto once they cross the Channel, as if they were crossing the boundaries and restrictions of their London existences.

On one tour we had to scrape two actors off the floor nearly every night, so there is good and bad in all nations, but at least we did have the actors. I suppose if you have no conscience you can do almost anything, and without the guilt that travels with it. You can take it to almost any lengths. Without a sense of restraint, man is reduced to the lowest and basest of animals, and the American system of no restraint and unbridled free enterprise does unfortunately appeal to the baser instincts.

Greek . . . London . . . 1988

It was just because Georgia Brown was in London that they decided to revive Greek. Time Out *requested an article which at the time I was happy to deliver. It is a thumb-nail sketch of the time and I was confirmed in my belief that little had changed since I wrote it a decade before. The reviews this time were a lot better than before and the audiences flocked once again.*

Well folks, it's been quite a season as we finish our epic twelve weeks of *Greek* playing to a small army of people. Approximately thirty thousand people of all shapes and sizes wended their way to Wyndham's Theatre united by one thing, apart from their desire to see *Greek*, and that was their youth. I have seldom seen such a turn-out for theatre when the vast majority was young, vital and alert. A sea of faces each night beamed in on us and took back our message, and the storm of applause cracked like thunder eighty-one nights. Outside in the three passageways surrounding us like a moat the tide of humanity spewed up their guts on Friday and Saturday nights and the noise crept in the doors like an invading plague of yobbo-joy and frolics, and yet inside Wyndham's there was laughter or silence. Without theatre we would be dead. Even a film is a dead experience. Rock concerts are mainly dead affairs since electronics amplify 95 per cent of what you hear and the rest is mush and persiflage, dished to umpteen thousands whose experience is a tiny dot wriggling in the distance. Theatre is the last temple of the arts. Just you and them. No amps. No embalming in celluloid. Just you and your sweat. Film is more overwhelming but only repeats the past, endlessly. So we performed *Greek* and watched life imitating art. The play's relevance in 1980 when I held up the same mirror to the warts and sores of our septic isle had become even more relevant in 1988. The sores had not healed but become more purulent and eventually almost incurable, as if we were on a one-way ticket to Palookaville. What I had fantasized had become reality. 'People are afraid to stroke each other's loins lest new laws against the spreading of the plague outlaw them.' Each week the world outside was catching up with the play inside, not that this was any astute Cassandra-like vision. Just remarkable that in the ensuing eight years nothing had changed. The bombing continued. 'My fucking husband's lying across the road, his legs on one side, his torso on the other.' The traditional football yobs, the natural outcrop of a deeply frustrated society, has flourished into sub-cultural heritage. 'The Scotties line the kerb face down in vomit which swishes along the rat-infested gutter, dumb jocks, down for their dozy game of football, any excuse to flee their fat and shit-heap Marys in the tenements.'

And why not? What else is being offered to a working-class man who seeks relief and a chance to get his rocks off? Every night *Greek* found its echoes in the outside world as our audience stepped over the bodies or ploughed their way through the drunks in St Martin's Court. They must have thought they had stepped into the play itself.

'Eddy's' solution was painfully simple. I had not just taken a sharp knife and plunged it into the swollen carcass of Britain and watched the bile pour out. I had also tried to recommend a cure. Love, being all-embracing, contains healing and enlightening elements that act as a curative. Also you cannot kick what you love either, and so Eddy's paean to the wonders of love reversed the guilt in the original Oedipus myth. Quite rightly the plague was a warning against the dangers of an incestuous society, but now the plague that infects us is one of indifference and hatred. But hatred is so satisfying for some for whom love is a twisted and repressive concept. The now fashionably derided hippie culture preached its easy mix of love and sex and was immediately suspect by those for whom love represented a threat to their upright stance. The hippie creed, on which I was more bystander than participant, was beneficent and humane. Their concerts, parties and protests were characterized by a lack of violence, which to them was an unintelligent and moronic reflex of a bourgeois society that is quick to go to war, quick to drop its napalm and fears anything that isn't in its own dead, unimaginative image. The bourgeoisie feared communism as well as free love which they, like the Nazis, somehow equated. So the first thing was to change the image of that society whose models were clean-cut, Hollywood-foisted. The hippies became hairy monsters fucking furiously and smoking joints, instead of swilling your lager, and indecently refusing to kill people in far-off places. What a devastating threat. For the first time in decades men actually looked beautiful and graceful. Women were exotic and felt liberated, and a new set of ethics and values rushed in. Unlike the punks who really are echoes of love-fearing neo-Nazis and who characteristically wear Nazi insignia, the hippies' models were totally unique in that they were an amalgam of Eastern, Aztec or American Indian.

In 1968 I began directing my first production of Kafka's *In the Penal Colony* at the Arts Lab in Drury Lane. The Arts Lab was, along with other venues sprouting up everywhere, to catch the creative emissions that seemed to be ejaculating from the minds of all and sundry. Never was there such a proliferation of ideas. Performances were diverse and eclectic and it was possible to see in a single day everything from mime artists like Kemp, performance artists like The People Show, Kafka, Jeff Nuttall, music, dance and movies. It was a museum of the bizarre, or rather a Mecca, and without the eccentric American ex-patriot Jim Haynes it could never have flourished. Hippie culture pervaded London in a riotous display that seemed to affect everyone and at the same time, underpinned by the sexual revolution, seemed to liberate people to be more honest and open in their performances. Now of course sex is a dirty word. It is a political act. Like age.

I recall the arsehole who wrote to *Time Out* letters and mentioned his age like kids do when they write – 'I am eight years old . . .' etc. – except that he said he was twenty-nine, as if this gave him some viewpoint of the world when his thoughts were as decrepit as if he were one hundred and nine. Age is something that happens to you, like herpes. It is not a skill. Age is a measuring rod for old-age pensions and killing in the army and that is its only relevance. The sixties was a generous age in that it embraced all ages. Its heroes were old and wise. Silver-haired gurus were as revered as Burroughs, Hesse or Leary, and while a strong element of fakery crept in there was a stronger residue of life-enhancing acts. A million courses sprang up teaching one how to think, be, eat, do yoga, tai chi, re-birthing, moving, breathing, and if some were charlatans the message was always the same, which was to break down the constipated bourgeoisie-regimented yea-sayer! HQ was the Round House in Chalk Farm, NW3, run by George Hoskins, and where we premièred Kafka's *Metamorphosis* in 1969, which followed the season of the Living Theatre, a bunch of itinerant actors from New York who had offended decent society and now were in permanent exile performing *Frankenstein* as a metaphor for the automata society. Olivier was running the greatest theatrical team in history and Nureyev was at his peak. The Beatles poured their narcotic mix of wit and syrup into our minds while John was the rebel who never spared the world his thoughts and contempt for the sickness of violence, little knowing that after his being shot by an ugly uptight slob some slug would crawl out of the woodwork and sneak into his underwear and write his turgid, muck-raking biography. That such a hack should be called an iconoclast is the supreme irony. In a sense the generation's fearlessness led to excesses but that was the nature of liberation. Even the symbolic manifestation of stripping off your clothes on a stage was still within the scope of the decontaminating process. The pioneers started and the administrations took over. The Round House was eventually destroyed by people who sought for West End transfers and the odd dollop of culture once a year. The famous bar which was a sanctuary for all elements was closed to the public since it attracted too many hippie 'bums'. In the end the Round House, which housed some of the most exciting theatre of the age, including four shows of mine, died. It was killed by people who loved the building but hated the people who had nourished it. The age gradually wilted and became rotten. The adventure palaces of Haynes and Hoskins were replaced by respectable venue-seeking 'Perrier Awards' and sanitized companies. I continued along my path anyway, since I was always on the sidelines, while perhaps being nourished by the greatest explosions of human imagination the twentieth century had ever seen.

Solitary in Tenerife . . . 1990

During a break in Salome *at the National I took off alone to Tenerife. I moved amongst the memories of an earlier time when I was there with my then wife, Shelley. As I walked through the small village I felt myself sinking into a deep reverie and identified the ghosts swirling round me. We were very happy in the village of Adeja but on revisiting it all had changed – for the worse.*

It's still there, the old white hotel
a single solitary worn-out star
adorns the lintel above the door.
I enter and it's just the same
the galleried hall, showers on each wing,
the room No.19 where we heard the waves
breaking over our dreams in single beds
the daylight crept under our sleeping lids.
And then your early morning voice like pearls
threaded one by one to make a song
that blends with sea and wind in the early morn
'wad ya feel like doing, breakfast first?'
Then the great mighty gorge was walked
Baranco del Infierno it was called,
That awesome dragon's maw we crawled
so slowly awed by nature frolics.
Gaping shadowed jaws splintering rocks
and dizzying peaks, sharp crevices
and through the day's hot stabbing rays
we gaped and sweated at the marvel of it
yes, we marvelled at the wonders of the world
we marvelled at our universe
since we were children in the spring of life
and loved the divine pictures God gave
our love-smote eyes and sang with joy.
One year we slept in an old house
where sweet young angels served us rolls
and coffee steaming in big cups.
I went down first to scrawl my words
to paint a verbal landscape of the past
a scrawl to heaven, the deepest thanks
for giving us a feast to toast our lives

and on the bus fatigued and worn
by charter flight in early dawn
we found the soft sweet bliss, my hand found yours
I was aflame in young male lust
excited by the shattered day
jet flight, new sights which broke the crust
the stale routine where habits lay,
beneath tumultuous throbbing seas
and heart-beats later we conjoined
in soft Canaries sand we hid our wine
to draw the chill from crashing waves
and thrilled to be swimming on Christmas Day.

Sixteen years later/Hotel breakfast

The couples creep in one by one
a solitary lady sits quietly
stirs her solitary tea-bag in a pot
a quivering mass of flesh attends
to take her order, 'toast or rolls?'
the waitress shifts her massive weight
from foot to foot while the lady thinks
'rolls please' she cries in plaintive tone
as if request might be denied.
Again I hear above the murmured sea
beneath the grey and scowling sky
the low dull tones of guilty couples
eating breakfast with joyless lips
almost conspiring to be alive
as if an unseen enemy would pounce
on decibels that roar too loud
that speak of life and energy
as if a guillotine would fall
upon those gushing throats and stop

Solitary in Tenerife: 1990

those tongues for evermore
and now her tea-bag slowly spirals down
her pink short-sleeve and *Daily Mail*
we toss a few words back and forth
'we'd never witnessed such grey skies
not for a decade seen such bleak
and cheerless days.' . . . Nephew in Ozzyland
confirmed the wettest summer of all times.
'Ay,' I purred with polite veneer,
'the world's thermometer is all awry'
it's hot and cold in the wrong lands
like my tomato soup heated by micro-wave
with scalding parts and parts lukewarm
reflecting nature in one small bowl
the artificial heat slams molecules around
while others miss the deadly ray.
'Take it back,' I cried, 'take it back.'
I fled into the street, still planted
with strident trees, thick trunks and leaves
to stop the sun melting your eyes
and shade bambinos in their prams.
I walked and walked forever down
an endless street of memory
to trace that one especial walk
where bananas grew in purple wombs.
Yes, found a path and climbed and fell
the plantation was still there, yes,
stumbled over stones and cried out
'Where's the path, the gentle walk
that meanders down my memories?'
I crumpled into dusty ravines
leapfrogged o'er streams from distant peaks
where soft thick clouds buff the edges
of their broken and jagged teeth.

Then at last after the crackle
of lizards flying from my steps
sharply sounding in the silent noon
I found the road to Calletas
and marched with sweating aching calves,
walked the gap twixt sea and torn-up sky
striding the past with rivulets of sweat
but satisfied, walked into the maelstrom
of the churned-sea, past solitary church.
We sat once counting the waves
until I found the stony platform
the sun-hot stage from whence
I plummeted into the heaving beast
where fishermen dragged silver tuna
packed so tight like rubber toys.
There was a café where every fruit-juice
of the world was there for you to taste,
try them all and take a picture by the door,
a red door in a cobalt blue wall
'This will be special' she said.
Now walked each step gathering up
the threads of memory, as Theseus
tracing the minotaur's maze, I wrapped it
around my mind like silk, and reached the
bay of Calletas, past cacti with red
bulging fruit whose pierced skin spurts
the colour of blood, past the sleeping
bananas like babies' hands.
The café's still there, same wooden chairs,
it's old and now neglected, selling beers,
no fruit-juice of every shade and taste
for curious lips and playful tongue,
now only beer for deadened buds
cruel lips and faggy breath

whose glasses pile up high on tables.
The sky has added layer upon layer
as if it was wasted on this sight
of mah-jong players whose swinish kids
search beneath stones for living things
to tear apart like plastic toys
while eating crustaceans, cracking shells,
the nails scoop in while making swinish yells.
Some voices have a northern tang,
I expect them to make jokes
any second break open a gag
about their mother-in-law or wife.
So I found the bay Calletas intact
sans fruit-juice of every taste
from guava, peach to cantaloup,
a newer café joined the bay
with cushioned seats and salads
served with tuna and fresh crunchy bread.
The heat now poured upon my head
and fed a sleek, strong, blue-eyed cat
grey as a rat, a perfect coat
responding to my outstretched hand
and then flopped down just near my chair.
From time to time, the way one does,
I stretched my fingers out just to touch
a living thing so pretty and so fine
while next door, they played mah-jong and smoked,
    the swine.
Finished my salad, mopped the juice
with broken crusts, the cat approved
and licked his chops and walked the aching
footsteps back, beside bananas,
once more I lost the fragile threads
and cursed myself, the route curled round

and found again the bouldered hill
to shudder up, foot by sliding foot
but thinks will keep the old boy fit
and left so gratefully my London sweat
until I found the road to Adeja
pronounced ARDECHHA, with a rasp on *ch*.
Walked through eight miles of memory
and saw you here and there and once you
kneeled to touch a young dead tuna.
I wandered in our past which cloaked
me like light rain.

Saturday 5 p.m. Rain/In Café

Don't sweat in fear and loathing, shame
to sit alone and contemplate your pain
compare with others drinking at one place
sharing tales, their weft and warp of life
each gives the other strands which then they knit
and form a verbal tapestry of it.
When you alone play all by yourself
a game of solitaire and bounce the ball
like those who play alone against a wall
your wall of memories, you beat again
and yet again the same old drum
you chew again the same old stew
of memories, except the taste is empty
in your mouth although it fills your
empty stomach for a while.
Illusionary food won't nourish
but keeps at bay the biting hunger in your heart
the way a cigarette will dull the pain
of hunger by deceit, so memories are smoke
to keep away the void that eats your heart away.

Solitary in Tenerife: 1990

Monday 10 December/The Café

Sat alone, it was OK, I chose fish
from out the fridge whose lid gaped open
like a jaw, the fish lay waiting
to be picked just hoping that its death
will justify its snatching from its salty bed.
The icy morgue was full of all the colours
of the sea, giant prawns and brute-red clams
and other massive slabs of flesh just lay.
I picked my partner for the night, 'It's white?'
I asked, 'like innocent of squelchy funny bits?'
'Starched-shirt' nodded sagely, 'si, esta bianco,'
sat down in the space where solitary people feast
who make companions out of dead fish and
other objects they can stuff into their mouths
to stop the emptiness and wordless hole,
they plug the soundless organ up.
Well it's not so bad, it's better than being bored
with an alien who only talks
the same old chords, and repeated, ad nause.
An old-faced man sat at the next grave
since solitary people may appear dead,
moving hardly and silent as a corpse.
The old man said in northern whine
'The weather's been absolutely foul,
mind you last Sunday it were good.'
(He was fighting against his role as corpse
and screaming 'I'm alive, I speak'!)
As if last Sunday was the grid in which
the sun must duly do its work,
the compass where the needle points to sun.
'Mind you, last Wednesday were good as well'
and thus he shuffled all the days

and picked out all the aces.
He liked the coloured photos on the wall
of fishes dressed up and adorned
with bright red peppers, onions and fat toms
those culinary images that line the walls
of restaurants that specialize in fish.
He'd like to own one of these, he said,
between the forkfuls as if he felt
the need to feed the spiritual side
in the intermission when his mouth
was full of steak and chewing hard,
'We all need art at times,' I said.
His wife's gone back, her mum's took ill
and so he sits in solitary gloom
watches the rain and eating steaks
so big he wraps up the remains
in a paper serviette for a dog
he made a friend of on the beach.
I crawled away, the fish was a beaut,
delicious and white and each bite,
each morsel was perfect, so thanks
fish, you did not waste your precious life
inside an ungrateful mouth that chewed
with no real pleasure or even joy
in some spoiled not quite hungry child
who leaves the best part of you behind,
you were my companion for the night.

This terrace is really perfect,
I never discovered it before

A dark void, black as pitch
with only the gurgling roar of the waves
only the white tongue of surf

and the lamps on the terrace walls,
only the lights bouncing off the waves
shimmering as a path of gold
like a golden snake it moves
carried on the spellbound sea
under the dark black empty night
starless, jet black, and milk warm.
A sangria pours its liquid balm
it comforts me, the god of wine,
just hear the whispers of the waves
pressing its breast on the sandy shore,
drags itself back to renew the quest
then endlessly returning to itself.
A white plastic table is my bench
wherein I hew and cut the words,
the altar wherein I offer my pain
and try by trial and error to define
where my world has failed me and mine.
A flashing star moves slowly in to land
carrying its cargo of live meat,
white porcine masks, fasten seat belts,
brandy is cheap in Los Christianos.
Let's go and sit in Canaria
and bathe in blood-warm seas and drink
and stagger the asphalt shop-lined streets
and read the *Daily Mirror* while we feast.
And what's the sun doing today,
the night-time discos pound their dirge
and birds in tight-white arse-filled tights
smoke fags, chew gum, and guys get pissed.
My waiter now bungs down the plate,
no word . . . nothing . . . no, not even
as in France, 'bon appetit', just that,
a little word would give the sauce

to coat your fried fish, chips and salad.
So then you ask, 'Excuse me, any salsa?'
'No!' He says, 'No!' . . . no extra words
to indicate regret, just no, no,
the largest gift of sound he is prepared
to give, and then you chew your fish
and chips with its big slice of tomato.

On the Wrecking of the Santa Monica Pier by Storm . . . 1983

Each morning, and starting from my first visits to Santa Monica, I would run and even attempt to skate to the pier. Once on its hot wooden planks I'd make my way to a charming little diner at the end of the pier where I had an unrestricted view of the sea to Malibu and the blue-grey hills of Santa Monica. I loved the end of the pier and this poem is a dedication to its demise. The end of the pier collapsed into the sea after a fierce storm.

The pier was smashed last night/
The storm chewed through and ate
The wood that held the rafters/
Held the mood of lingering smells
Of summer and the spell of sunsets
That so slowly fell while you on elbows
Cupped your face and leaned against
The old pier's washed-out frame/
The crest, the crown, the head
Was chopped just where you leaned
And lines were spent in hope/
Of hooking from the deep a living
Fishy thing/ a storm sent crashing
Tons of seething beating fists and
Smashed the old and aching timber/
Shuddered, cracked and groaned
Heaved and split, leaned over dragging
Down the dreams/ the buckling and
Split seams and knelt like old
Boxer stunned from pounding blows/
And then like slow, it shuddered
Sank and died into the deep and cold/
And waves buried an old and shaggy
Head/ its warm and sun-drenched planks
Where all the hopeful feet did stomp
And stamp/ the wives with tattooes
Threw their lines with cruel hooks
And husbands squint their eyes
And coffee's drunk and DJs squeal
Their stuff from steel cassettes
And kids would scream and shells
Were cracked for things to use as

Bait, the stink of dead and fishy
Slimed the deck and lazy talk would
Float into the blue and hazy hue
Mixed up with saccharine old songs
Which wooed the throng who cracked
The afternoon with coffee, hamburger
And cool silk breezes lifted skirts
And guts, beer-swelled, hang over belts
And I drank coffee with a tuna melt.

And watched the sun-spilt seas
Wrote poetry and felt the blood
Begin to rise when a line of mine
Did hook a rhyme and up it flew
All wet and flapping coloured in
Hues from fathoms deep and scrawled
Its sleek and new-born soul in
Words across my page and shoals
More sweet did tumble in my net
I crushed my teeth into the tuna
Melt where Japanese or Viet did
Fry the breakfast for old guys/
With hats and peaks and old ladies
Said 'more coffe, sure'/ I gripped
my pen/ ate up the hills and tore
The seas into salt lakes
That formed small pearls
In corners of my eye when
Sky and sea poured endlessly
And ate the fish and drank
The coffee and said thank you
'You're welcome' came the swift
Reply/ and ventured out where
Sky-stretched clouts of puffy

Cloud and mounds of flesh leaned
Smoked and waited for the sea
To leap in shape of wiggly salty
Things/ and then at bloody end
When sun dripped iron in the sea
And made a blood-red fantasy
And folks thinned out and giant
Pelicans did scout for flesh
Thrown up by kids who loved the
Jaws that snapped and trapped
Sardine or thing too small to take
Then one dark raging night giant
Waves did curl their mits and
Fought the ageing trembling legs
That gave up sagging, no blame
Can be attached or stain can
Blemish its old head where poems
And fresh fish did fly and birds
Cut shadows from the sky and old
Men leaned against your thighs
And children cried and I, yes I
Would ask for tuna melt/ and when
You died old pier I, yes I, let
Out one huge and heavy sigh.

The Run . . . New York . . . 1990

This time I had an appointment in New York to meet with a director and so I wasn't booked in my usual Gramercy Park Hotel but one near Central Park. It's weird running in Central Park and feeling the city closing in on you from all sides, but it is also fascinating and this is an impression. I didn't get the part, it was a screen version of one of Doctorow's less successful books, but at least I did renew my acquaintance with Dustin Hoffman who had just played Shylock in New York.

Take myself into the humid sultry morning air of New York in August at 6 a.m. Walk from my hotel to Central Park and even the park seems weird and menacing, its dark foliage thick and threatening in the morning's heat. The park's divided into so many sections, dells, vales, rotundas, and secret small copses, that it makes a perfect environment for sex or murder or any of the nasty things that people do to each other with some regularity in this overwrought metropolis.

The park has an atmosphere to me of mystery, as if it were in some way enchanted with both fairies and with evil goblins. It seems appropriate to initiate one's entry into New York with a sweaty jog around Central Park to purge the poisons out after a long flight. The joggers are already pounding the asphalt but unlike your regular British jogger, who seems a standardized shape, here they come in all shapes and sizes; wheezing, puffing, shunting, fat ones, old ones, Japanese fat old ones, young fit ones, girls with Walkmans in their hands, others with them strapped to their shoulders. So I follow a line of joggers up some small hills and down a long path, which meanders and splits up, taking the joggers off into the directions of their choice according to the length they have allotted to oxygenate their brains sufficiently to be super-alert for the day in the office. The morning air is heavy with the perfume of the park, an odorous compound of all the trees excreting their smells during the tepid night, a pungent and slightly sweet odour that you quickly recognize as a New York summer smell. The park was originally a rather dank and fetid wood and marshland that was reclaimed and redesigned into the area it is today, a perfect oblong and the one great sanctuary in New York, although that has not been particularly its role in recent history.

My sweat pours out easily. Before I started I grabbed a coffee from a local diner, where even at 6 a.m. two men are engaged in the kind of open-lunged banter that draws a thin line between invective and jest, and one of the combatants has already stepped into the arena of aggression while the other is trying to keep it on the other side of mockery . . . I took my large paper cup into the park as a throat-wetter before getting going. The wall surrounding the park is just waist height and defines the lungs of Manhattan but it is also the bowels, the doss-house and its psycho ward. Green jungle or sweet park, dotted with teen kids playing baseball. At night you can hear Shakespeare for free under the balmy air and the current offering is *Taming of the Shrew* but now the actors are sleeping after their successful night and the mandatory celebratory drink or dinner, where actors like to recap and dwell on their self-obsession since it has now vanished into the Central Park air or is lodged within the memories of the audience, who are scattered to the four winds.

There's a kind of pride when you think that a thousand people watch you each night, but the pain is that you have to do it all over again. So they turn in their beds all the more lonely not having a thousand pairs of eyes on them. I take my coffee and sit on the bench contemplating my run and the city. Each bench is occupied by a tenant, who is not a down-and-out tramp but an ordinary poor citizen, and they are mostly black or Hispanic. One man is sleeping in his suit, while his shoes wrapped in a plastic sheet make his pillow. A Latino lies with a small radio on his chest blaring out a Spanish station. A middle-aged black lady is just rising and pulling on her pants and is indifferent to the niceties of bourgeois modesty, since there are no walls or bathrooms to protect her. Others are still sleeping since it's warm and pleasant and they won't freeze to death as many did last winter.

The park is sultry and balmy but the green is relentless, almost metallic; nothing light green, or yellow or white. Mostly sycamore and all sturdy and bushy, a healthy dark dusty green with no relieving shade or tone, and the wall is uniformly a dull ochre. The sleepers stir in their isolation waking with no applause ringing in their ears unless they are woken by the thunderclap that rings out after the performance each night in the Delacorte Theater. The name sounds like a cake, as so many American institutions do for some reason, like the Dolittle Theater or the Mitzi Newhouse, while the names we give our theatres like the Lyttleton or the Cottesloe are suitably dull and meaningless.

The 'bums' or the homeless awake to a fairly hopeless existence and stare wanly at the curtain of steel and concrete that seems to surround them like an implacable enemy that has crept up during the night. The windows of the skyscrapers stare down over the park with utter indifference, like cold deadly giants that consume their quota of human flesh each day, washing them down with vast amounts of the city's energy and spewing out the worn-out remnants at night. The buildings stop at the park as if they have come to a halt like an advancing army. From the park they could be the sides of cliffs, mountain peaks, jagged chasms. From your green shade you are surrounded by a power that bespeaks of energy so awesome it seeks constant building and growth and, reaching higher, pushing itself into the firmament, stalagmites emerging within cracks until the light is shut out, shaped like chisels or like spears. The older turn-of-the-century skyscrapers were built in gradually receding squares, one atop another like a telescope you keep pulling out, and on the top are small Gothic-style villas floating in the air with their turrets and castle-like crenellations. Gargoyles leap out of their sides like they were giving birth to panthers and these were put there to protect the buildings from evil spirits.

The heat hangs in the air as you run, pushing one heavy-laden thigh in front of the other, and you jog away those worries that hang like small weights, like some handicap to slow you down. So run to release the sleeping endorphins, the euphoria that will soon spread through your body. I run and follow yellow shorts for a while since she appears to know the route and I keep her steadily receding bum in my headlights. Cars are instructed to turn right at East 72nd Street. Some rocks break through the earth like prehistoric broken bones. The horizon starts to change and as I run I wonder where the woman was attacked and gang-raped and beaten almost to death last year as she unwisely took a night jog through innocent trees and shaded groves.

I pass the park's 'features', an old-time dairy where a group of figures are beginning to stir, and I pass near the Dakota Mansion where Lennon had his poor skull shot out and the building looks as menacing as its history. In front of the Dakota is a shrine, a small piece of the park movingly named 'Strawberry Fields'. Years ago, in the seventies, one didn't dare enter the park after dusk and legends grew that spoke of the most awful things happening to you if you dared cross into the dark inferno, and the power of the legend grew to the extent that people feared even walking next to the walls lest hands would shoot out and grab them or their bags. Here in the square of darkness murder takes place, a healthy six-foot yuppie ties up and murders a young woman and with yuppie predictability pleads self-defence. 'She squeezed my balls . . . !' Poor girl, strangled within the smells of chestnut trees and beech, within the sounds of Shakespeare's words wafting through the air. Shakespeare's plays have humanized the park since now it is visited at night by hundreds of people eager to see famous actors re-acquaint themselves with the bard.

This was the inspiration of Joe Papp, New York entrepreneur, genius, show-biz wizard, producer of *Chorus Line* and *Hair*, and part-time singer. So hundreds of people leaving the theatre each night is a formidable army against muggers and an area of the park is returned to civilization. I finish my jog and feel a different being from the one who started just twenty minutes ago and, as I leave the park, the sleepers are still clinging to their solace.

Junk Travel . . . 1990

I was in Fiji making one of the most horrendous films of my life, allegedly about the secret early life of Errol Flynn – on my way back I decided to change my ticket and go via LA, since I couldn't resist the opportunity to revisit, thence on to New York. The unbelievable story that follows is an example of how a certain airline loses millions each year. Be warned.

LA Airport – Pan Am counter. A young clerk examines my ticket, keeps staring at it as if he were solving the theory of relativity; he looks sallow and efficient. Then, like a frenzied Rubenstein attacking Chopin, he performs a two-handed attack on the computer. The answers are not coming up and he is not getting the right tune. I merely want to revise my flight and change destination using my bona fide ticket, paid for and collected at the Pan Am offices in London. He stares again at the ticket as if hoping that the few numbers he has to deal with will magically reveal a hidden truth. He again attacks his most favourite machine on earth. He looks like he is aiming for the jackpot. His fervour and excitement suggest to me the now unpleasant idea that, like a cop, he wishes for a conviction. He is searching for a fault! He is hunting down some infinitesimal clerical error that will not only allow him to flaunt his power and prevent me from travelling, but demonstrate to his masters what a vigilant watchdog they have employed. My mind has put its warning lights on and starts making its own computations. I have placed him on the waiting list for a job with the Gestapo. The queue behind me grows but he continues to punch the computer and nothing will deflect him from his search for some impurity in my ticket, even if the queue extends till Doomsday. I turn round guiltily to the waiting passengers who are tired or are carrying kids and they look at me as if I should leap out of the boat and save the sinking craft.

He again stares mindlessly at the ticket and I know now that he is not very bright, in fact fairly stupid, since by now he must have gleaned every bit of info on the ticket and is staring into the vacancy of his own head. It's obvious he is playing for time and so he begins his initial interrogation. 'How much did you pay for it? How was it paid? Where?', although all the info is on the ticket. 'When did you travel?', although this has nothing to do with anything since he now disappears to consult his oracle, the supervisor. He reappears looking as if he has just performed a childish deed in the school toilets and says smugly that the supervisor will be out in a moment. 'What's wrong with the ticket?' I at last venture to ask. His eyes narrow and, like a good member of the CIA, he intones: 'This ticket was issued illegally, you can't use it.' I have now relegated him from the waiting list for the Gestapo to chief interrogator of undesirables. His insides must be tremulous with the possibility of making a kill. 'But,' I protest, 'this ticket was issued in London by Pan Am and if you made a mistake then it is *your* mistake and you must rectify it.' His tone implies that Pan Am are illegally working some scam in London, whereas what he really means is that there might be a mistake, a clerical error, but his vindictive and paranoidal brain is programmed not to use words like 'mistake' with reference to his employer, and he has to resort to the terminology of the law or police. I had actually renewed and upgraded a year-old ticket in Pan Am in London, a routine and everyday occurrence. His voice drones on with its simple repetitions that all bureaucrats intone when their brains become incapable of analytical thought and rely on a few clichés from the manual. 'It cannot be my problem,' I say, 'since the mistake, if there was one, was made by Pan Am.' Then, bereft of any other evaluation of the problem, he comes up with the oldest canard in the book when the brain has gone into final decline: 'It's more than my job's worth', as if this minor and alleged error is of such huge gravity that only the severance of this nasal android could recompense for the outrage. Then, having taken the drama to the level of personal sacrifice like a good little Nazi, he adds, 'I like my job', to which I can only reply that *I* don't like his job. His tones are now taking on a whinging sound like someone who has been bullied at school for informing. His snively 'I like my job' in that nasal whine is turning me off America since I am detecting more and more creatures of the State, impotent wimps who shelter themselves in bureaucracy and love nothing more than making life difficult for people.

I now wish to get out of a place that produced such specimens. He disappears yet again and now reappears with a scrappy old tart who is off the mark like a whippet and has, no doubt, been fed with some nice distortions of the rude British customer. She is primed to show her snivelly android how to deal with me. He follows her out, trying to wipe the last vestiges of a snigger off his yellow face. I am now convinced that the Pan Am staff at LA Airport are not prepared to solve the problem but actually have a deep-seated need to cause pain and discomfort. Not once have they made an attempt to help, solve, aid or treat me like a valued customer whose services and future patronage they are hoping to secure. 'Can't use this', the supervisor warbles, her voice grating with authority. 'This was issued illegally' and thus echoes her underling's phrase that he must have tossed into her mind when he went into her sanctum with the good news of his discovery. Holding on to my cool, I reiterate the obvious, that if it is a mistake then it is Pan Am's fault and they must take the responsibility for any error in the ticket since *I* hadn't made out the ticket, I had merely paid for it. She seems to yield slightly to my protestations and now, coming more under my influence than the wimp's, she will, as a last resort, explore one last avenue and ring 'New Jersey', 'but it will take a while' she promises. No apologies, no regrets or concern, I am treated like someone trying to make a con. After fifteen minutes she returns and somehow reluctantly admits that it is usable. Yes, it was cleared by 'New Jersey', but she feels she is doing me a big favour.

Right, now that my ticket is OK I no longer wish my neo-Nazi interrogator to have anything more to do with the handling of my ticket and step over to the next clerk whose seniority in rank is evident by a chest festooned with badges with images of aeroplanes on them. He is elegantly coiffed and somehow sees himself as if on a stage as a leading man. 'Would you please take over my ticket?' I plead. 'The supervisor has now ratified my ticket . . . I've been here nearly *one hour!*' 'No you haven't' he exclaims, as if he cannot believe that anyone could be kept waiting an hour and then be found to be right. I have been here fifty minutes. 'Bring your cases here,' he snaps curtly, as if I am somehow still a criminal who has got off with a good lawyer. He cannot bring himself to acknowledge that ghastly, sweaty aggravation, accusation and final reprieve since a mistake is too much to admit, so I still have to be treated like a criminal. The new leading man plays his computer with more skill and soon has a print-out of a new ticket which could have been done in five minutes in the first place. Now over an hour has passed and only when I see my luggage go safely through and disappear along the long rubber tongue that will soon be ensconced in the belly of the plane, do I venture to make a comment. 'You know, I've been here over an hour and my ticket was proved to be valid and yet not once did anyone offer any degree of apology or hint of concern. And if there was a small error it was your Pan Am office in London that caused it.' He seemed momentarily at a loss for his cue, and like an actor who has forgotten his lines, his face seems to sag while his computer scans the distant past for the appropriate response and in the end his best is: 'We can only go by the ticket.' At least it is marginally better than 'I like my job'.

Up on the plane I happen to pick up an issue of *Fortune Magazine* which lists the health of each airline, economically, that is. Pan Am is way down the league with losses in 1989 of £336 million. I wonder why?